D1381118

800 055 230

Diesel Pioneers

David N. Clough

Ian Allan
PUBLISHING

Contents

First published 2005

ISBN (10) 0 7110 3067 7
ISBN (13) 978 0 7110 3067 1

All rights reserved. No part of this book may be reproduced or transmitted in any form or by any means, electronic or mechanical, including photocopying, recording or by any information storage and retrieval system, without permission from the Publisher in writing.

© Ian Allan Publishing Ltd 2005

Published by Ian Allan Publishing

an imprint of Ian Allan Publishing Ltd,
Hersham, Surrey KT12 4RG.
Printed in England by Ian Allan Printing Ltd,
Hersham, Surrey KT12 4RG.

Code: 0511/B1

Visit the Ian Allan Publishing website at
www.ianallanpublishing.com

Front cover top: **SR-designed 1Co-Co1 No 10201 at Dorchester South in May 1952.** *S. C. Townroe / Colour-Rail DE628*

Front cover bottom: **Ex-LMS Co-Co No 10000, in later Brunswick green livery, breasts Camden Bank with a down local train in June 1962.** *J. G. Ewing / Colour-Rail DE18*

Back cover top: **English Electric Co-Co prototype No DP2, in later two-tone green, prepares to leave Leeds Central for Bradford Exchange with the down 'White Rose' Pullman in February 1967.** *G. W. Morrison*

Back cover centre: **Brush prototype No D0280** *Falcon* **enters King's Cross with the up 'Sheffield Pullman' in 1962.** *Colour-Rail*

Back cover bottom: **Rebuilt with GEC-Ruston engine, Class 37/9 No 37905** *Vulcan Enterprise,* **in Railfreight grey livery, stands in Severn Tunnel Junction yard in March 1987.** *G. W. Morrison*

Title page: **Renumbered 1200,** *Falcon* **prepares to leave Paddington for Weston-super-Mare in June 1972.** *G.F. Gillham*

Introduction

The adoption of diesel as the source of power for main-line traction on Britain's railways is an intriguing subject. Inevitably, politics played a significant part in events. Britain had a strong heavy engineering and manufacturing industry that was willing to invest in demonstration locomotives for BR to evaluate. There were also sufficient such companies to ensure healthy competition when it came to component options. In consequence, nine different designs of engine, some in various stages of development or cylinder arrangement and ranging from 800 to 2,300bhp, were trialled during the transition from steam to diesel, more than on any other European railway.

The era of the passenger locomotive is now in its twilight, with an ever-increasing number of multiple-units displacing hauled rakes of coaches. The railway industry in this country has also seen a revolution of similar magnitude since the heady days of the late 1950s, when mass dieselisation was embarked upon. Many works have closed, notably Vulcan Foundry and Swindon, and names such as Beyer Peacock and North British Locomotive Company are but memories.

This book concentrates purely on main-line locomotives, excluding shunters, while gas turbine locomotives are left out because they run on kerosene, not diesel fuel, and have a turbine, not an engine, as the prime power source. The aim has, therefore, been to concentrate on the various phases of dieselisation, considering the designs that emerged, their sphere of operation and degree of success. At various times BR held the honour of having the world's most powerful locomotive running on its rails: *Deltic* was the most powerful single traction unit in 1955, while *Lion* held the honour of the most powerful single-engined locomotive in 1962, a mantle subsequently taken by HS4000 *Kestrel*.

Many sources have been researched during the preparation of the manuscript. Unfortunately these do not always agree about certain facts. When this is the case, the most reliable one has been used, while in other cases the differing versions are given. The tables of particulars have been compiled, so far as these have been available, from the 1966 edition of the BR locomotive Diagram Book. Manufacturers usually ascribe their own internal numbers to locomotives constructed, and while the generic term 'works number' is used, the builders did not all follow this nomenclature; for example, North British Locomotive Company referred to them as 'progressive numbers'.

Acknowledgement is due to several people. Mike Hunt and Geoffrey Hurst have contributed towards aspects of the research, while Mike also made a number of insightful suggestions while proofing the text. Peter Meredith, who served for many years as part of the LMR's M&EE Department, has given information covering his own experiences with a number of the locomotives dealt with here, particularly No 10100 and the

Metropolitan Vickers Type 2s, on which he was the BR representative throughout the refurbishment programme. Peter Waller, Ian Allan Publishing's Book Publisher, contributed significantly in assembling the photographic selection. Except when in the company of other locomotives, the pictures selected depict only prototypes or members of the Pilot Scheme orders. Following this stricture has made compiling the illustrations much more difficult, particularly in finding examples from the early days before prototypes were re-ordered as production batches. Finally, as always, I am most grateful to my wife, Jo, who has suffered as an author's widow and then proofed the manuscript.

David Clough
Leigh
April 2005

Bibliography

BR Diagram Book MT25, 1966 edition

Clough, David N. and Rapson, D. I. *Locomotive Recognition Class 37s* (Ian Allan)

Clough, David N. *Class 50s In Operation* (Ian Allan)

      Type 5 Freight Diesels (Ian Allan)

Cock, C. M. *The Deltic Locomotive* (Proceedings of the Institution of Electrical Engineers, December 1958)

Locomotives of the LNER Part 10a (Railway Correspondence & Travel Society)

Marsden, C. J. *British Rail Main Line Diesel Locomotives* (OPC)

Nock, O. S. *Sixty Years of West Coast Express Running* (Ian Allan)

Reed, Brian *Diesel-Hydraulic Locomotives of the Western Region* (David & Charles)

Tufnell, R. M. *The Diesel Impact on British Rail* (Mechanical Engineering Publications Ltd)

Tufnell, Robert *Prototype Locomotives*

Webb, Brian *English Electric Main Line Diesel Locomotives of British Rail* (David & Charles)

      Sulzer Diesel Locomotives of British Rail (David & Charles)

      The Deltic Locomotives of British Rail (David & Charles)

Issues of *Diesel Rail Traction, Trains Illustrated, Modern Railways, TRACTION, Railway Magazine* and *The Railway Observer*

1 Pre-Nationalisation Prototypes

Sir W. G. Armstrong, Whitworth & Co (Engineers) Ltd prototype

This was the first main-line diesel locomotive to run on Britain's railways. It was a diesel-electric with a 1-Co-1 wheel arrangement, built in 1933 as a speculative venture by Armstrong Whitworth under Order Number DT8. It had an Armstrong-Sulzer 8LD28 engine, running at 700rpm and producing 800bhp without turbocharging, the unit being manufactured by Armstrong Whitworth. Sulzer's LDA28 power plant (in turbocharged form, hence the addition of the 'A' in the nomenclature, being the first letter of 'Aufladung', the German word for turbocharged) would feature significantly over the following 30 years in the evolution of diesel traction in this country.

The main and auxiliary generators were supplied by Laurence, Scott & Co Ltd of Norwich, while the three self-

Pictures of the prototype built by Sir W. G. Armstrong, Whitworth & Co (Engineers) Ltd are rare by virtue of its short life. This official view is dated 13 November 1933 and shows that it carried no running number. *Ian Allan Library*

ventilated axle-hung traction motors were supplied by Crompton Parkinson Ltd of Chelmsford. Full engine output was available between 6 and 65mph. Engine starting was electric, using an 80bhp Armstrong-Saurer (not Sulzer) oil engine-dynamo set in the bonnet. Radiator fan drive was by a Davidson-Aerto electric radiator fan motor, which was thermostatically controlled. Provision was made for up to three locos to work in multiple. Livery was black and no running number was carried, although it was given the works number D9.

By agreement with the London & North Eastern Railway (LNER) the locomotive worked a demonstration run from Newcastle to North Wylam and back on 6 July 1933. Further testing took place later in the year between Newcastle and Berwick, and also on the Carlisle line. It was officially received on trial by the LNER on 19 February 1934. On 7 June it worked a special passenger run for members of the Institute of Transport from their conference at Leeds to Darlington Reclamation Depot and return. All other workings were with goods trains, frequently between Newcastle and York. A minute of the LNER Locomotive Committee dated 28 June authorised a further four-month extension of the trials. During its trials 26,140 miles were run and fuel consumption worked out at roughly 1 gallon per mile.

Armstrong Whitworth prototype	
Length	39ft 10in
Width	n/a
Height	12ft 8in
Weight	72 tons
Wheel diameter	
powered	4ft
non-powered	3ft
Engine	Armstrong-Sulzer 8LD28
Engine output	800bhp at 700rpm
Max speed	70mph
Tractive effort:	Maximum 28,500lb
Continuous	n/a
Gear ratio	n/a
Fuel tank capacity (gallons)	n/a
Minimum curve radius	n/a
Works Number AW D9 of 1933	

An engine crankcase explosion in June 1934 brought an end to the prototype's career. Ownership had always been with Armstrong Whitworth and, in view of the LNER's lack of interest in taking the prototype further, it was never repaired and languished at the builder's Scotswood Works until eventually scrapped in 1937.

London, Midland & Scottish Railway prototypes Nos 10000 and 10001

The London, Midland & Scottish Railway (LMS) had dipped its toe in the water with diesel traction as early as 1927 when it produced a 500hp diesel railcar that employed an English Electric (EE) diesel. A year later it produced a 400hp diesel shunter that used a Paxman VXS engine. In 1934 the LMS again collaborated with EE in building a 350bhp shunter, which became a standard design. Again, EE supplied the power plant — a six-cylinder version of its 'K' range design that had a 10-inch bore. This earned itself a good reputation for reliability, and an ability to run for long periods between overhauls.

Once World War 2 was over, the LMS determined to take the lead among Britain's railway companies in main-line diesel rail traction. In May 1946 the Railway's Chief Mechanical Engineer, H. G. Ivatt, and Sir George Nelson of EE agreed on a joint venture. The railway's works at Derby was put in overall charge of the project, handling design and construction. The official order was Derby LMS Order No 2510, while Lot No 198 was also issued and the English Electric equipment supplied was under that company's Contract No 6T0566. Several factors influenced the design. Notable among these was the British loading gauge, which was smaller than its Continental and American counterparts.

Design evolution was further influenced by limitations in the available height within Derby Works for lowering the diesel engine into the locomotive body. To overcome this the sides of the locomotive had to be made removable, and this meant that they could not be

What appears to be a view of No 10000 under construction in Derby Works. *Ian Allan Library*

load-bearing structures. In turn, this forced the use of a heavier underframe than was possible subsequently, which brought the need for a Co-Co bogie. Credit is due to the Derby design office, which produced a very good result. EE experienced some problems in developing the 16-cylinder version of its SVT engine, which was derived from the RK 10-inch bore range; it was not delivered until May 1947. EE also supplied the generators and traction motors. The main generator was an EE823A, rated at 1080kW, 1500A, 720V, at 750rpm. An EE909A auxiliary generator was rated at 44kW, 340A, 130V, over the range 350-785rpm. Six EE519/3B traction motors, rated at 260hp, 550A, 400V, at 805rpm were used.

Following American practice, cab nose ends were added, but these contained only a compressor and traction motor blower. Nose-end gangway doors were fitted to enable intercommunication with a second locomotive or the train; however, these doors where rarely used and were always a source of draughts in the cab. Livery was black and silver. It was highly commendable that the overall length was only 61ft 2in, far less than other prototypes, with an overall weight of 130.6 tons. The maximum axle load was 22.2 tons, which was less than the largest LMS Pacifics; however, with an installed power of only 1,600bhp from its diesel, its tractive capability was some way below that type. In fact, the LMS assigned a 5MT power classification,

whereas the Pacifics were 8P. Maximum tractive effort for the diesels was given as 41,400lb.

No 10000 made its debut on 8 December 1947, less than a month before Nationalisation brought the LMS's existence to an end. Sister No 10001 did not emerge until July 1948. Meanwhile No 10000 had been trialled between Derby and Manchester, followed by express passenger turns between St Pancras and Derby from the spring of 1948. On these it proved to be the equal of the Class 6 'Jubilee' steam locomotives. It is interesting to recall the reticence with which footplate crews reacted to the new arrivals. The seniority system meant that men had to wait until fairly close to retirement before graduating to express passenger rosters, and this meant that they did not adapt well to change. One

Derby driver continued to lean out of the cab side window during the entire run up to London with a diesel, just as he would have done on a steam locomotive! The ride was very comfortable, if slightly springy.

From October 1948 Nos 10000/1 took up West Coast duties, based at Camden steam shed. Later that year the duo moved back to the Midland line until the Summer 1949 timetable, when they returned to the West Coast.

During the next few years the pair were used both singly and in multiple on the main Anglo-Scottish services. Prevailing schedules were undemanding and overall time could be kept with a single locomotive, except on the 'Royal Scot'. Transferred to Willesden, Nos 10000/1 were deployed from Euston to Blackpool, Crewe and Liverpool.

Above left: **The first couple of years of operation saw the LMS prototypes spend time on both the West Coast route and the Midland main line. On 1 March 1949 No 10001 passes Kegworth heading the 12.3pm Derby to St Pancras train.** *J. F. Henton*

Left: **Most of the West Coast route express passenger diagramming involved both Nos 10000/1 working in multiple. The duo pass Rugby No 5 box on 2 September 1950 with the up 'Royal Scot'.** *H. Weston*

Above: **During their early years, unreliable steam generators for train heating caused the LMR prototypes to be restricted to freight use during the winter. In 1952 No 10001 approaches Tring summit with a down goods.** *Lewis Coles*

Top: **While working on the SR, No 10000 has charge of the down 'Royal Wessex' on 2 July 1954, seen here between Salwood and Eastleigh.** *Brian Morrison*

Above: **This picture of No 10000 at Derby, dated 30 September 1956, is included to illustrate a variation in livery: note the absence of the silver body band and a pronounced silver roof.** *A. W. Martin*

Unreliable steam heating equipment tended to restrict passenger operation to the summer months, but during the winter there was no shortage of freight traffic to move.

O. S. Nock published details of a journey behind No 10001 in *Sixty Years of West Coast Express Running* (Ian Allan). The trip was in 1950 on the 9.10pm London to Glasgow sleeper, which nominally ran non-stop, but called at

Carlisle Kingmoor for a crew change. With a trailing load of 525 tons, rear-end banking was not taken out of Euston up Camden bank, but was used on Shap and Beattock. Speed reached 61mph at Watford Junction, passed 2 minutes early in 24m 5s. This rate fell away to 53 over Tring summit and thereafter the general pattern was the use of full power on uphill stretches, with an easing when going down grade.

Demonstrating the traffic intensity even late in the evening, there were several bad signal checks before Preston, as well as slowings for track work. Notwithstanding these, and with a 67mph top speed, Preston was passed less than 2 minutes in deficit on the 261-minute booking. Hard work was done as far as Tebay, where there was a further signal stop. Grayrigg was cleared at 29mph, so it is unlikely that Shap would have been tackled unaided. Nevertheless the calculated power output was roughly in line with the locomotive's 1,600bhp rating. Top speed down to Carlisle was 74mph, but signals again intervened and the crew change was made 12 minutes late.

Thereafter the maximum was 69mph twice and a creditable ascent made of Beattock. Here the train was accelerated to 28mph, compared to only 23mph on Shap, both, of course, banked. Glasgow Central was reached a few minutes late overall but with a gain of 6.5 minutes on the 141-minute schedule. It is inconceivable that a Class 5 steam engine would have put up such a performance over such a distance.

EE certainly benefited from having two mobile test beds for its SVT engine. Although of minor effect on performance, the leaking of oil from cylinder head and crankcase covers gave rise to a dirty engine. This, of course, was something of a discouragement to maintenance staff who had to work on the engine. Fuel injection equipment, timing chains and turbochargers also gave varying degrees of trouble.

By far the main problem experienced, though, was with the train-heating boiler. This item of equipment was to prove something of a Jonah for BR diesel traction over the next two decades, and was frequently the cause of locomotives being failed. Understandably, winter deployment was on freight diagrams between Camden and Crewe. During this sphere of operation, fuel consumption per ton-mile was calculated to be 0.015lb, which should be compared to the figures given later for the Southern Railway locomotives. While operating these freights, it seems that full power was used for most of the way.

Southern Railway prototypes Nos 10201-3

Despite planning to electrify all its main routes, the Southern Railway (SR), under Chief Mechanical Engineer O. V. S. Bulleid, and its Chief Electrical Engineer, C. M. Cock, prepared a design for a main-line diesel-powered traction unit. Ashford Works was assigned construction of the first two locomotives, with Brighton Works being responsible for the third, all under SR Order No 3441, which did not start until 1949. Axle load limit was set at 18 tons for two reasons. First, the Southern had considerable experience of the effect that small-wheeled bogies, with axle-hung traction motors, had on damaging the track; reducing the axle load would lessen the track stresses. Second, a low axle load offered greater route availability and therefore more operational flexibility.

Based on the LMS's experience, this meant a four-axle bogie would be needed, having three axles powered and the leading one unpowered. The resultant design proved successful and was a feature employed in the designs for the large diesels that came out of the 1955 Modernisation Plan. Another change to the LMS design philosophy came at the cab front, where the Southern adopted a flat profile. Drawing on American experience, one of the arguments for a nose end was to cut down the effect of 'flutter' from the sleepers, but the Southern did not believe this to be the case. No provision was made for connecting doors in the cab front, which were always a source of cab draughts in locomotives so fitted and were little used.

EE was contracted to supply the major traction components, engine, generators and traction motors. By this date the 16SVT diesel was fitted with Napier turbochargers, in place of the Brown Boveri type used previously. Added to other improvements, the rating became 1,750bhp. Gearing of the EE519 traction motors was a high 52:21 to provide a top speed of 110mph — this was with a view to introducing a high-speed service

Right: **Two official views of No 10201, displaying its length, together with the 1-Co bogie. Low marks awarded for styling!** *Ian Allan Library*

Below: **An interesting study of No 10202 taken at Waterloo before departure for Exeter with a Plymouth service on 3 December 1951.** *Brian Morrison*

The SR-designed prototypes were intended for the former LSWR main lines from Waterloo to Bournemouth and Exeter. On 8 September 1952 No 10201 sweeps under Battledown flyover at Worting Junction with the 1pm Waterloo to Plymouth train. *Brian Morrison*

between London Waterloo and Exeter and Bournemouth.

Interestingly, the radiator fan was driven by an electric motor, rather than by a direct drive from the free end of the engine. The radiator shutters were thermostatically controlled, a feature that was not replicated on later designs, apart from Class 50. Engine-room air came through dry pack Vokes filters, whereas general practice at the time, and for many years thereafter, favoured oil-wetted filter units.

No 10201 ran a trial trip from Ashford to Ramsgate and back in December 1950. Final adjustments and painting into a black and silver livery followed, with more trial trips to Rye and London Victoria between Christmas and New Year. On 4 January 1951 No 10201 was handed to the London Midland Region (LMR), based at Derby, and over the next two weeks it ran trials between London St Pancras and Manchester Central. The 1 in 100 gradients over the Peak Forest section overtaxed the traction motors at the prevailing gear ratio, causing

excessive temperatures. Returned to Ashford on 17 January, it was repainted and then spent nearly a year being exhibited at the Festival of Britain, not re-entering service until February 1952.

Sister machine No 10202 emerged from Ashford during August 1951. After initial trials in Kent, it went to Nine Elms shed (the main-line depot for Waterloo) for driver training. Originally the Southern had planned to base its diesels at EMU depots in order to provide more appropriate servicing facilities than could be offered at technologically primitive steam sheds. Clearly in the post-Nationalisation era there had been a change in policy.

No 10202 entered revenue service on 25 September 1951 on the 11.54am Waterloo to Salisbury train. Subsequently it worked trains from Waterloo to Bournemouth and Exeter, running between 3,400 and 4,120 miles per week. While at the head of the 1pm to Exeter at Waterloo on 15 October, a turbocharger bolt fracture was spotted by the EE riding technician. To avoid a failure, he spent

Above: **The last of the SR trio, No 10203, approaches Worting Junction with the 'Atlantic Coast Express'.** *EE*

Right: **The SR also deployed its diesels on selected services to the Kent Coast, as evidenced by No 10202 on the 'Golden Arrow', captured on 13 February 1954 on the Bickley to Petts Wood loop line.** *Brian Morrison*

the trip sat astride the hot main generator, feeding oil into the damaged turbocharger!

Keen to see the potential for a high-speed West of England service, a demonstration run with a five-coach load at up to 100mph was arranged for 24 October. Unfortunately the plans had to be revised as a result of connecting rod

fractures on the new 'Britannia' 4-6-2 steam engines, because the Railway Executive did not want the attendant publicity attaching to high speeds. Instead eight vehicles were taken from Salisbury to Waterloo with a stop at Andover. The 17.3 miles to Andover were covered in the 22-minute booking. Onward to Waterloo, 66.2 miles, the 63-minute timing was cut by just over 1 minute. Top speed was given unofficially as 92mph near Hook.

In late April 1952 the WR dynamometer car was used for detailed performance assessment, when loads of up to 432 tons were taken on the Exeter line. Drawbar efficiency was established as 18.63% and a lower gear ratio for the traction motors was recommended. This was changed to 65:17, but an extra stage of motor field weakening was added to give a better high-speed characteristic in compensation. Further tests were carried out in October, which showed that re-gearing had increased tractive effort by 23% at 20mph, caused no change between 35 and 50mph, but reduced it at 70mph. Maximum recorded value was 37,820lb, against the 48,000lb predicted.

No doubt based on its experience with No 10201, the LMR did not commandeer No 10202. Instead, on 29 October, the locomotive commenced a four-leg daily diagram that started at Waterloo with the 1.25am newspapers to Exeter. Returning to London on the 7.30am train, this was followed by the 1pm down and the day ended at the head of the 5.53pm from Exeter. No 10201 came from exhibition in January 1952 and also went to Nine Elms. The work assigned during the year varied between express and semi-fast services from Waterloo to Bournemouth, Weymouth and Exeter.

By now Brighton Works had assumed responsibility for the diesel fleet. Not only was it handling the work on the third locomotive, but the prototypes were also far from trouble-free. A range of technical problems emerged in relation to the turbochargers, fuel pumps and cylinder heads, together with field winding failures with the main generator and traction motors. All these provided useful experience for EE and fulfilled the objective of prototype trialling, namely to eradicate design faults. Despite these difficulties, the locomotives were achieving annual equivalent mileages of nearly 80,000, roughly the same as Classes 45 and 47 during the 1980s.

No 10203 appeared in March 1954, with a number of design changes. EE had uprated the 16SVT to 2,000bhp; this was achieved by a higher top speed of 850rpm (compared to 750rpm), cylinder

So that's where the water goes! From an era when water columns for steam locomotive tender replenishment were a feature of stations, No 10202 is probably having its steam generator tank refilled. *W. M. J. Jackson*

heads with four valves (instead of two), and larger Napier turbochargers. Improvements to the governor permitted continuous torque control of the engine. A different main generator, the 10-pole EE822/1B (rating 1313kW, 1750/1545A, 750/850V, at 850rpm), and a different traction motor, the 6-pole EE526 (rating 202hp, 565A, 300V, at 393rpm), were installed. Curiously, No 10203 weighed in some 3 tons less than its cousins at 132 tons.

Initial trial runs were between Brighton and Tunbridge Wells. Allocation to Nine Elms from April was followed by exhibition at the International Railway Congress, staged at Willesden, between 25 May and 4 June. Thereafter most of its work was on the Exeter route, save for a week on the 'Golden Arrow' between London Victoria and Dover in March 1955. In June and July of that year, with an accumulated mileage from new of 106,000, dynamometer trials were staged. In broad terms, these produced results in line with predictions and established No 10203 to be a coach superior to No 10202. Interestingly, the more powerful machine also proved to be marginally more fuel-efficient than its older cousin at 0.023lb/ton-mile, against 0.0248. Despite a nominal rating of 2,000bhp, the calculated output during the trials of the 16SVT diesel was only 1,883bhp.

The data for the two diesels tested have been compared with results for an un-rebuilt Southern 'Merchant Navy' Pacific, as set out in the accompanying table:

Tractive effort (lb) on level track			
Speed	No 10202	No 10203	Steam
30	17,000	18,000	19,000
50	9,000	10,500	12,000
70	5,000	6,600	8,000
80	3,000	4,500	6,000

Note the superiority of No 10203 in the higher speed range, albeit eclipsed by the steam locomotive. Whether the latter was an everyday reality, as opposed to a special stunt with a hand-picked steam locomotive and crew, is a matter for debate. Nevertheless, no one would sensibly claim that even No 10203 was a match for a Class 8 Pacific. At 30mph No 10203 was developing 1,440hp at the drawbar, while at 70mph it was 1,200hp.

Based on these results, it was not surprising that the Southern Region opted out of large diesel procurement, preferring to retain its modern steam fleet until electrification of key routes was completed in 1967. By way of comparison, the results with No 10203 were matched with results from similar controlled road tests at the same time with a WR 'King' class steam locomotive. The 173.8 miles between London Paddington and Exeter with a 500-ton load were estimated as 163 minutes for the diesel and 169.5 for steam. Of course, No 10203 was assigned a 6P/6F power classification, which seems rather low. Based on runs by a later design that had the same power equipment (BR Class 40), this locomotive was fully equal to the sustained maximum effort of a Class 7 steam engine; an argument can be made that in everyday service No 10203 was equal to typical Class 8 steam efforts of the period.

The appearance of two prototype diesels on the Southern Region had brought the decision in the spring of 1953 to allocate all four machines there, no doubt to concentrate experience and operation. Prior to taking up their duties from Nine Elms, Nos 10000/1 both visited Brighton Works for overhauls, having completed nearly 400,000 miles. This was roughly the interval at which Type 4 diesels were shopped during the 1970s and 1980s.

No reliable record of the availability of the quintet has been published. It seems unlikely that any, apart from No 10203, would have been entrusted with the principal expresses to the West Country, though there are reports of utilisation on the 'Bournemouth Belle' Pullman. At one date in early 1955 only No 10001 was in traffic. By now the SR had decided to abandon large diesel traction units for principal expresses, so the five machines

gradually made their way to the LMR. No 10001 was the first to move in February 1955, where it found work on Euston to Bletchley locals, based at Willesden shed. April witnessed the transfer of Nos 10000 and 10201/2. Perhaps surprisingly, the last two appeared on their own on the up and down 'Royal Scot'; such were the demands of the schedule at that time that

a locomotive of Class 5 could be assigned the task. No 10203 finally arrived at Willesden, after its dynamometer car tests, on 20 July 1955.

The year 1956 proved to be a poor one, with long periods spent out of traffic. A highly relevant factor here was EE's lead-time in supplying spares, especially for the Mark 1 engine fitted to Nos 10000/1

According to the photographer, this was the first appearance of No 10201 on a Derby to St Pancras service, observed at Wellingborough on 15 August 1956.
G. W. Morrison

and Mark 1a to Nos 10201/2. This, again, was to be a frequent issue during the 1970s and 1980s with EE-equipped locomotives. All bar No 10203 acquired an all-over BR green livery, with No 10203 following later. No 10000 had a silver line, No 10001 had white numbers and a duck-egg-blue line, and the others sported orange and black lining.

With up to five units available, the Operating Department diagrammed the diesels on services from Euston to Wolverhampton, Manchester, Glasgow and Perth. The 5P machines appeared in multiple on the 'Royal Scot', whereas No 10203 was allowed on its own. Arguably the best period of availability during this phase was between 1 January and 30 September 1958. However, official figures show that the performance was relatively poor:

While the mileages run were most creditable, the availability figures were not. It seems that the fleet was deployed on long high-mileage turns, on which they would be much better suited than steam equivalents. Downtime, however, marred potential. By way of comparison, the best steam locomotive class during the same interval proved to be the former LMS 'Duchess' class Pacifics. Although these managed 69% availability, the average mileage was a mere 56,800 — honours therefore to the diesels, when compared to the best steam performers.

The road performance potential of a nominal 6P machine can be judged from a 1959 effort by No 10203 between Rugby and Euston on a Wolverhampton service. Trailing a typical nine-car consist, it covered the 82.6 miles in 68 minutes at 72mph, with 95 attained near Wembley. No 'Jubilee' steam locomotive ever managed this. Operations gradually shifted to local passenger turns out of Euston and Broad Street after 1959. Before that, though, the January 1959 issue of *Trains Illustrated* compared No 10203 against an 8P 'Duchess' Pacific. On the up 'Royal Scot' from Glasgow, No 10203 trailed 480 tons, against 475 tons for No 46221. Plugging away up the Clyde Valley through the Motherwell area, the diesel fell to 37½mph on the rising

**Availability performance (measured in days),
1 January to 30 September 1958**

Loco	Works	Depot	Traffic	% available	Mileage
10000	70	43	148	57	80,636
10001	76	48	155	56	83,861
10201	62	30	181	66	104,532
10202	44	39	190	70	111,514
10203	84	35	135	53	74,865

Table of annual mileages and days out of service (OOS) for the Southern prototypes

Year	No 10201		No 10202		No 10203	
	Miles	OOS	Miles	OOS	Miles	OOS
1950	773	1				
1951	2,508	297	41,517	4		
1952	114,052	127	120,571	119		
1953	119,433	106	72,245	166		
1954	95,689	147	84,847	162	72,574	63
1955	42,842	182	45,197	182	71,462	152
1956	13,424	262	6,805	278	31,682	227
1957	146,370	82	149,122	78	110,795	90
1958	79,791	131	86,262	118	69,360	159
1959	46,534	173	41,351	195	30,226	205
1960	46,699	123	32,946	150	64,366	59
1961	33,311	118	13,877	226	11,355	216
1962	8,006		33,907		6,639	

1 in 100, and 1,570rhp was developed, matched exactly later in the journey when ascending Whitmore bank south of Crewe. Such an effort represented a full 2,000bhp engine rating and matched the work of the steam locomotive. In fact, unlike steam, the diesel maintained the pace down grade as well and confirms the view that a diesel locomotive of this type was fully the equal of prevailing West Coast schedules and everyday 8P Pacific performance.

No 10001 was the last to undergo an overhaul at Derby Works. Here the diesels made too-regular visits for unscheduled repair between 1960 and 1962. With squadron production of new diesels by this time, these prototypes became misfits. Nos 10201/3 were dumped in Derby Works yard in late 1962 and were joined by Nos 10000 and 10202 early in 1963. Official withdrawal came in December. No 10001 survived until March 1966. How reprehensible that all were sold for scrap in 1968.

Being the most powerful of the five, No 10203 was allowed to handle the 'Royal Scot' on its own. This is the up service at Acton Bridge on 2 August 1957. *S. D. Wainwright*

Nos 10000/1

Length	61ft 2in
Width	9ft 3in
Height	12ft 11¼in
Weight	131 tons
Wheel diameter	3ft 6in
Engine	EE 16SVT Mk I
Engine output	1,600bhp
Maximum speed	90mph
Maximum tractive effort	41,400lb
Gear ratio	55:18
Fuel tank capacity	900 gallons
Minimum curve radius	4½ chains

Nos 10201-3

Length	63ft 9in
Width	9ft 3in
Height	13ft 1in
Weight, Nos 10201/2	135 tons
No 10203	132 tons
Wheel diameter, powered	3ft 7in
non-powered	3ft 1in
Engine, Nos 10201/2	EE 16SVT Mk 1a
No 10203	EE 16SVT Mk 2
Engine output, Nos 10201/2,	
continuous	1,600bhp
1-hour	1,750bhp
No 10203	2,000bhp
Maximum speed, Nos 10201/2, original	110mph
revised (SR service)	85mph
No 10203 (SR service)	85mph
Maximum tractive effort, Nos 10201/2, original	31,200lb
revised gearing	48,000lb
No 10203	50,000lb
Continuous tractive effort, Nos 10201/2, original	14,000lb at 37mph
re-geared	21,500lb at 21.5mph
No 10203	30,000lb at 19mph
Gear ratio, Nos 10201/2, original	52:21
revised	65:17
No 10203	61:19
Fuel tank capacity, Nos 10201/2	1,150 gallons
No 10203	1,180 gallons
Minimum curve radius	4½ chains

No 10800 and *Hawk*

The LMS did not confine its main-line diesel aspirations to the large type that emerged as Nos 10000/1. Something smaller in the 3P power category was also ordered, but with this prototype the railway company subcontracted the design and construction to the North British Locomotive Company (NBL) under the latter's Order No QP (Queens Park Works) 977. The layout of the locomotive, which was given the running number No 10800, was very similar to an American 'road switcher'. Starting at one end, there was the cooler group (radiators and radiator fan), next came the power plant (engine and generator set) and train-heating boiler. A single cab followed this, with a stub nose at the other end that contained the control cubicle. Locating the cab in this way gave better bi-directional visibility than by having a single cab at one end.

Davey Paxman & Company (Paxman) supplied the engine. This company can claim the first British railway application

Evidence of the silver paint used as part of the original livery is seen in this undated view of No 10800. Note also the trademark diamond NBL worksplate above the number.
Ian Allan Library

No 10800 was deployed on both passenger and freight work while allocated to the LMR and SR. On 15 April 1953 it brings the 10.18am Brighton to Victoria train into Isfield. *T. J. Dadswell, Cecil J. Allen collection*

of a diesel, as its VXS model in six-cylinder form, developing 412bhp at 750rpm, had been chosen by the LMS in 1928 for the latter's prototype 0-6-0 diesel shunter. For No 10800 an RPH model engine, in 16-cylinder configuration, was selected and provided 827bhp at 1,250rpm. Coupled to this was a British Thomson Houston (BTH) main generator, accompanied by a BTH auxiliary generator. Four BTH traction motors were axle-hung on the Bo-Bo bogies. Overall weight was just under 70 tons. Top speed was 70mph, and the maximum tractive effort was given as 34,500lb. Livery was black and silver, with silver being used for the bogies as well as the roof. Silver bogies soon showed the dirt, however, and these components quickly received the more customary black paint style.

Design and construction proceeded slowly and No 10800 did not emerge from NBL's Glasgow Works until May 1950.

Initial proving was carried out in Scotland before acceptance by the LMR on 17 July, allocated to Willesden shed. On 14 November a press run was made from Euston to Watford Junction. Suburban traffic out of the London terminus as far as Bletchley occupied the locomotive for the next two years. Mirroring events with the large diesels, No 10800 was sent to the SR for trials in July 1952, but based at Norwood Junction shed. Reports suggest that it was generally used on London Victoria to Oxted services, though it did appear on the Region's South Eastern Division and was also noted at Brighton. On these passenger turns it was being matched against Class 4 steam traction, nominally a class higher than the designation of No 10800.

From December 1954 No 10800 was given to the Eastern Region (ER) at the East London shed at Plaistow, where the main work performed was on local transfer freights. Plaistow also provided motive power for services from London Fenchurch Street to Southend, and the prototype was tried on the commuter trains on this route. However, clearly the ER saw little use for No 10800 because it went back to the LMR in February 1955. Based at Rugby shed, its main tasks seem to have been on cross-country passenger and freight services, which took No 10800 east to Cambridge, west to Oxford along the line from Bletchley, and north to Birmingham.

Service experience was poor. The main problem was the Paxman engine. The cylinder heads were of the 'Comet' pre-combustion design and did not produce a clean exhaust due to poor combustion when linked with a turbocharger. The poor combustion caused fouling of the turbocharger exhaust turbine and this reduced engine performance by restricting air supply. Attempts to remedy this problem were made by advancing ignition timing, but this caused high peak cylinder pressures, which then brought frequent cylinder head cracking. At one stage cylinder heads were being replaced at the rate of almost one per day. NBL's engine cooling system was deficient in

that it was prone to the formation of steam pockets, which did not help engine performance. Given these problems, it is surprising that No 10800 survived until 1959, when it was withdrawn on 8 August. It had, though, provided valuable experience to both the manufacturers and regional operating departments.

For the majority of discarded locomotives, that would have been the end. Brush Traction Company was starting to examine the technology associated with AC power generation for locomotive propulsion. At that time all diesel-electric locomotives produced DC power from the main generator and this was fed to DC traction motors. Rotating the generator's armature shaft inside its fixed field coils produces a current, which is transmitted through carbon brushes that touch the copper of the armature.

While this system is relatively cheap, and offers efficient power conversion (from the power produced by the diesel engine that rotates the armature to the amount of resultant electricity), it has limitations. First, the interface between brushgear and commutator becomes prone to flashover at power levels above

No 10800 is pictured towards the end of its BR days at Derby on 8 June 1958. *B. K. B. Green*

that produced by a 2,700bhp diesel. This limit of commutation therefore imposes a ceiling on the power that a single engine locomotive can supply. Second, the brushgear produces carbon dust, and removing this, with regular attention to the brushgear itself, requires maintenance. If the dust is left in situ, it can cause flashovers and these can cause fires; bad flashovers have been known to totally destroy a main generator.

AC power generation offered advantages, not least that an AC traction generator need not have brushgear, which of course removed the upper ceiling on power generation. Taking the process a stage further, AC induction motors could be substituted for DC traction motors. Technological limits at the time represented the biggest challenge because electronics were very much in their infancy.

Brush therefore saw No 10800 as a suitable test bed for AC power technology. Having bought the locomotive in 1961, the first action was the removal of the Paxman engine. At the time Brush was finalising a large diesel prototype, No D0280 *Falcon* (see Chapter 6) and had a spare Maybach MD655 diesel. This was capable of producing 1,400bhp at 1,500rpm and was a suitable power unit for the new prototype, which was named *Hawk*. Brush fitted an AC traction generator that gave a continuous output of 950kw, 600A, 1,325V, at 1,500rpm. This suggests a conversion efficiency of 91%, assuming that the diesel was rated at 1,400bhp.

Hawk's technology reached the stage in 1964 to allow the locomotive to be reassembled. BR lined green livery was adopted and the original running number added, though the name was not. In April

After purchase by Brush for experimental use, No 10800 is the centre of attention during a visit to Falcon Works by the Institution of Locomotive Engineers.
Ian Allan Library

1965 BR accepted the prototype for mainline trials and it went initially to the test plant at Rugby. Subsequently it ran on the former Great Central main line between Leicester and Nottingham where it achieved 65mph. This stretch of railway was, of course, convenient for the inevitable return visits to the Brush factory at Loughborough. By 1968 the electronics fitted were outdated and further development finance was not forthcoming. Having languished in Brush's works until 1972, No 10800 was cut up, with the engine being retained as a possible standby generator for the works.

No 10800/*Hawk*

Length	41ft 10½in
Width	9ft 2in
Height	12ft 9½in
Weight	70 tons
Wheel diameter	3ft 6in
Engine, as built	Paxman 16PHX Mk 2
as rebuilt	Maybach MD655
Engine output, as built	827bhp
as rebuilt	1,400bhp
Maximum speed	70mph
Maximum tractive effort, as built	34,500lb
Gear ratio	66:15
Fuel tank capacity	300 gallons
Minimum curve radius	3¾ chains

The notation on this official view of the newly completed Fell diesel-mechanical locomotive quotes its number as '10,100'.
Ian Allan Library

The Fell locomotive, No 10100

During the 1940s and 1950s several propulsion systems coupled to a diesel engine were tried. Among these there was only one attempt at producing a main-line diesel-mechanical locomotive, and this was No 10100. It was a collaboration between three parties, the LMR, Fell Developments Ltd and Shell Petroleum; the design was the brainchild of Lt-Col L. F. R. Fell, while Shell's involvement came in the form of development funding. The LMR provided design and construction facilities at Derby under Derby Order No 3610, and Lot Number 206 was also issued.

Just when Lt-Col Fell came up with the concept is unclear, but he formed his company and entered into an agreement with the LMR in 1948. The region's CM&EE, H. G. Ivatt, was instrumental in facilitating the project. No 10100 embraced three fundamental principles. First, the diesel-mechanical system aimed to eliminate the internal losses in both diesel-electric and diesel-hydraulic propulsion, whereby only between 75 and 80% of engine power was actually available at the wheel rim. Second, the multi-engined arrangement drove through slip couplings and differential gears. Finally, a variable boost was applied to the engines so that a high boost

Prior to final assembly, one of the gearboxes is mounted on a pair of driving axles while inside Derby Works. *Ian Allan Library*

at low speed produced high torque, with reduced boost at high speed.

Conceptually No 10100 was a 4-8-4 or 2D2, with nose ends and two driving cabs. A further change from normal practice was locating the main propulsion engines in the nose ends; these were four 12RHP Paxman diesels, each rated at 500bhp at 1,500rpm. Two AEC A210D six-cylinder diesels, each producing 150bhp at 1,800rpm, drove the Holmes-Comerville turbochargers, as well as other auxiliary functions; mounting was between the cabs. Both sets of engines used the same turbochargers, so the AEC units were also subject to variable boost.

This was certainly a novel design concept and offered several advantages. As with any multi-engined vehicle, failure of one engine did not cripple the locomotive. By using a high-speed diesel type (1,500rpm maximum), the weight of each was lower and more compact. Lt-Col Fell decided to use high turbocharger boost at low speed to generate the maximum possible pulling power for starting heavy trains and climbing steep gradients. This led to a requirement for a design of engine that responded flexibly to different rates of boost and did not give

rise to unduly high peak cylinder pressures. Whether the choice of the Paxman RPH diesel was because it offered these benefits, or because there was really no British-manufactured alternative, is open to conjecture.

Of course, as a mechanical drive, engine and road speed were correlated. This meant that at low road speed, engine rpm was low, and this explains why a high boost was required to give high power. As road speed rose, so did engine rpm and thus the power developed. By reducing boost, engine power was supposed to remain constant across the road speed range. At maximum engine speed, boost dropped to zero. At starting, only one engine was used, the other three cutting in progressively until all were powering by about 24mph. Each engine had a hydraulic coupling to permit this progression.

All four engines drove through a common mechanical transmission that used differential gears of David Brown manufacture. Three differential gears were employed, two being primary and one secondary, the former connected to the latter. The secondary differential carried the combined power through a gear train to the driving wheels, which were coupled in pairs. Adopting this system of differentials meant that a progressively changing speed ratio was achieved without the need for a car-type gearbox.

A curious benefit of this, possibly, ingenious design was that the maximum tractive effort was achieved at starting when, of course, only one engine was in use. Thus the failure of up to three of the RPH units would not prevent No 10100 covering any part of its duties, albeit at a lower speed, because there would always be sufficient tractive effort to move the train. This is not the case with diesel-electric propulsion, as witnessed with HSTs, which required assistance in Devon if only one of the two power cars was operating.

The regulator was part of a pneumatic control system that was fed from the same vacuum system as the train brakes. One of the initial design failings was that this system was inadequate and No 10100 could not cope with heavy trains at first, because of inadequate train brake vacuum. A radiator was positioned at the extreme end of each nose and was driven by the AEC auxiliary engines; one radiator coupled to one of the pairs of RPH engines and one of the AEC engines. Two boilers were provided for train heating.

The driver had six controls for locomotive operation: a regulator, a reverser, and four small levers that actuated the hydraulic couplings for each engine. With all six (four driving and two auxiliary) engines idling, the driving technique involved first opening the regulator, then operating one of the four levers to connect an engine into the drive train. The regulator was adjusted to determine engine loading. As the speed reached predetermined levels, other engines were actuated by moving their corresponding levers; these speeds were 6mph for the second engine, 17mph for the third, and 24mph for the fourth.

Some two years after entry into traffic, No 10100 departs from Loughborough Midland on 20 March 1952 with the 12.5pm Derby to St Pancras service.
Bryan S. Jennings

After trials on the Settle & Carlisle line during March 1954, No 10100 heads for Crewe with its test train.
J. E. Wilkinson

Top speed was quoted as 78mph, though in practice this seems to have been 72mph.

Compared to the diesel-electric prototypes under design and construction at the time, No 10100 progressed quite quickly and emerged from Derby Works in 1950 (sources suggest both July and December), painted in black with a silver roof and lining. Despite an overall length of just 50 feet, the nose ends were not long enough to permit an engine to be removed easily by a vertical lift. Testing and trials commenced in the Derby area, but in January 1951 a reversing dog clutch seized; oil samples taken at the time found lead/bronze present, suggesting bearing trouble. By May No 10100 had amassed only 100 miles, but it was taken to Marylebone for exhibition. In September a Shell technician called to check lubrication levels but was told that it had been done. Regrettably a misunderstanding had occurred, because it was No 10001 that had been checked. No 10100 was taken for a run along the Midland main line and reached Kettering before oil starvation caused a major failure due to bearing seizure.

Prior to, and after, this failure, the locomotive was deployed on St Pancras to Manchester Central passenger turns. Having clocked up 35,000 miles, in July 1952 a small securing screw in the secondary differential dropped into the reversing wheels while No 10100 was travelling at 50mph, causing considerable damage. During the first six months, the biggest cause of unserviceability was failure of the coupling rod bearing. This was alleviated by removing the centre rods, thus making the locomotive a 4-4-4-4 or 2BB2. By now a revised livery had resulted in the BR 'lion and wheel' emblem being applied centrally on the bodyside.

Initially the fuel tank had inadequate venting and this caused a partial vacuum during running; the effect was fuel starvation, despite the tank containing several hundred gallons of fuel. This prevented a London to Manchester round trip being made without refuelling and the tank was topped up by hand at Derby station on the return leg. Adding extra vents resolved this.

Dynamometer trials were conducted

Passing through the South Manchester suburbs near Didsbury, No 10100 heads a Manchester Central to Derby service on 12 January 1954. *Nigel Dyckhoff*

during March 1954 over the Settle & Carlisle route. These showed No 10100 to be capable of hauling a 385-ton train up a 1 in 100 gradient at 50mph, an achievement beyond what No 10203 of equal installed power could achieve. Between about 27 and 65mph, the Fell could outperform both its diesel-electric counterpart and also a BR 'Britannia' Pacific. Above that speed, power at the rail fell away very sharply to a very low value over 70mph, a factor that did not make the machine suitable for the high-speed passenger duties for which it had been designed. At 43mph the drawbar horsepower (dbhp — ie after allowing for moving the locomotive itself) was as high as 1,895, and this fully supports the design philosophy of a diesel-mechanical drive, yielding high transmission efficiency. Gearbox efficiencies were 95% at 36mph and 99% at 68mph.

The trials found that the four RPH diesels were developing up to 2,230bhp. Fuel consumption, at 0.56lb/dbhp, was very close to No 10203's 0.54 figure. Thereafter there is disagreement as to its sphere of operation. One source cites confinement to semi-fast duties between Derby and Manchester Central due to inadequate train-heating capacity. Another reports continued use between St Pancras and Manchester Central. In any event, on 15 October 1958 a fire at Central

caused severe damage and No 10100 was dumped at Derby until cut up in 1960.

It ran only around 80,000 miles, a disappointing total, probably due to the major failures it suffered. The lower boost pressure at higher speeds seems to have meant that the RPH engines caused less trouble than the unit installed in No 10800. The locomotive's operating life, though, was too short to form a conclusive view. Not to be overlooked is that, all told, there were 60 cylinders to potentially cause trouble. Plans by Fell Developments Ltd for a 2,300bhp version never got beyond the drawing-board.

The Fell locomotive

Length	50ft
Width	9ft
Height	13ft
Weight	120 tons
Wheel diameter, powered	4ft 3in
non-powered	3ft 3in
Engines, main	4 x Paxman 12RPH
auxiliary	2 x AEC 6-cylinder
Engine output, main	2,000bhp
auxiliary	400bhp
Maximum speed	84mph
Maximum tractive effort	25,000lb
Gear ratio	Not relevant
Fuel tank capacity	720 gallons
Minimum curve radius	5 chains

NBL Progressive Number 26413

The photographer of this December 1954 shot gives the location as Manchester Victoria. In truth, No 10100 is almost certainly at Manchester Central, where it ultimately met its demise when it caught fire on 15 October 1958.
P. F. Winding

Deltic

At the time of their design, the LMS and Southern prototypes were based on the most powerful diesel power plant then available. Construction methods available to the designers resulted in very heavy locomotives, which had low power-to-weight ratios. The combined power of Nos 10000/1 was equal to the limit of a Stanier 8P Pacific steam engine, and thus above everyday sustained performance, but the pairing together weighed considerably more than the Pacific. The deadweight of the diesels therefore cut the power available for pulling the train. Of course, this deadweight had a use in providing brake force for stopping the prevailing freight trains of the period, most of which were unbraked, aside from the brake-van.

An official portrait of DP1 *Deltic*.
EE Traction

With dynamometer car and modified coaches that generated a resistance against motion in tow, *Deltic* is captured in attractive Eden Valley countryside during trials on the Settle to Carlisle line. *EE*

In the post-war, post-nationalisation environment, Britain's railways were faced with the problem of improving their services in order to compete with better road transport options. In addition, extra traffic had to be handled, while there was pressure to reduce costs. Heavier and faster trains were called for, which needed more available horsepower. The designer had parameters in which to work, notably axle load and track curvature radius. The LMS prototypes had high axle loadings but all the wheels were powered, which benefited adhesion. In contrast, the Southern prototypes were constrained by the Civil Engineer's (relatively low) axle load, so had an unpowered axle on each bogie to spread the weight; this reduced adhesion and made slipping more of a potential problem. Overall locomotive weight also rose.

The LMS and Southern prototypes used medium-speed engines, a term used to denote a maximum rpm in the 600-1,000 range. With a view to raising the overall locomotive power-to-weight ratio, EE therefore considered the use of engines with a higher speed that could deliver more power for a given engine weight. A further benefit would be derived from the reduced weight of the mechanical parts (frames, superstructure, etc) that came from having a lighter diesel power plant, which is quoted as a ton saved on the engine weight permits a ton less to be required for mechanical parts. Lower locomotive weight per 1,000 horsepower would naturally reduce track maintenance costs and, theoretically, operating costs. What was required was a high-speed engine that was suitable for rail traction application.

D. Napier & Sons Ltd was an EE subsidiary. In response to a request from the Royal Navy in 1946 for a lightweight/high-power diesel for patrol

boats, it had produced an opposed-piston engine that was based on a German military design. This naval engine, the D18-11B, had 18 cylinders and had a 1-hour rating of 2,500bhp at 1,500rpm. Overhauls were required after 1,000 hours.

Clearly, for rail application an overhaul interval of around 6,000 hours would be needed to fit the maintenance cycle that brought the need for tyre turning around that time. Napier carried out testing and settled on a rating for rail traction of 1,650bhp at 1,500rpm continuously, and the resultant engine was the D18-12A. While the output per cylinder was only 90hp, compared to 110hp for Nos 10201/2, the overall weight of two D18-12As was only 20,130lb, against 40,800lb for the 16SVT in 10201/2. Combining two 'Deltic' engines, of course, meant that 3,300bhp was available, not 1,750bhp, and this offered a rival to the high-speed

diesel engines being developed in Germany for rail application in conjunction with hydraulic transmission. Obviously, EE was keen to use its electrical machines as the form of transmission, so fitting 'Deltic' engines meant that a locomotive could be built to rival the high power-to-weight ratio of the diesel-hydraulic.

EE's Bradford-based Traction Division ordered the new prototype from EE's Preston Works on 20 November 1951 as a speculative venture against Contract Number 6B2000 of 20 November 1951. Napier agreed to provide three power units free of charge. It seems that the different parts of the EE group regarded *Deltic* as a shop window that might tempt overseas railways to invest in a lightweight but high-power locomotive. At the time construction was completed, *Deltic* was the most powerful single-unit locomotive in the world. Originally

Deltic made its passenger debut on Liverpool Lime Street to Euston services. In this pre-electrification view of Lime Street station a crowd of platform-enders await its departure. *EE*

planned to be named *Enterprise*, the name was used first by another manufacturer, so *DP1* (Diesel Prototype 1) was initially coined, but later revised to *Deltic*, after its engines.

Preston undertook detailed design and assembly, although component manufacture (such as the engines) was shared between other locations as well. Each D18-12A engine (three were supplied, one as a spare) had a six-pole EE831 main generator attached. Interestingly, when taken out of service one generator was of type EE831A, while the other was an EE831/1B, which means that there is a slight design difference between the two. Connected in series, each generator had an output of 1,080kW and featured duplex lap windings to offer better commutation at high speed. The four-pole auxiliary generator was mounted in saddle fashion above its main generator.

The space between the engine-and-generator sets was used to accommodate the train-heating boiler. Such a location was not conducive to good maintenance, while it was unsurprising that the secondman did not welcome attending to it during service running, when the engines would be very noisy. Unusually, each engine had two radiator fans that were roof-mounted and driven mechanically by the same shaft that turned the auxiliary generator.

The underframes and superstructure were fabricated as a complete load-bearing structure to provide the body shell. While the main elements of the body were of substantial construction, light alloy material was used elsewhere (eg cab doors and roof panels) to save weight. An EE526A six-pole traction motor was hung from each of the six axles, giving a Co-Co wheel arrangement for the two fabricated bogies, the latter being similar to those under Nos 10000/1. Two stages of motor field weakening were employed in conjunction with a gear ratio of 61:19, which gave a 90mph top speed. This ratio was later considered too low and was changed to 59:21, giving a 105mph top speed. Sanding equipment was provided. After the first power controller position, the driver had notchless power control. Initial movement of the power controller did not alter engine speed but instead altered main generator excitation.

In a paper delivered to the Institution of Electrical Engineers, C. M. Cock refers to the design as evolving during

Above left: This undated photo finds *Deltic* passing Milford & Brocton, south of Stafford, on an up train for Euston. *EE*

Left: Deltic is again seen south of Stafford on a Liverpool Lime Street to Euston duty. *EE*

Above: The exact provenance of this scene is unknown – however, EE did attempt to interest the Canadians in the design. *EE*

By the time this view of *Deltic* was taken on 26 March 1958, EE had secured the order for 22 production series examples. The locomotive curves off the viaduct over the River Mersey between Runcorn and Widnes, heading for Liverpool on a train from Euston. *EE*

construction. Clearly the project provided valuable experience to EE in diesel locomotive design, which was to stand it in good stead later. On completion in October 1955, *Deltic* moved to EE's Netherton Works on the outskirts of Liverpool for static testing. A striking livery of powder blue was chosen for the bodysides, with two parallel yellow lines that ran the full length between the nose end grilles and came to a point there. Impractically, white was chosen for the roof, while bright yellow 'speed whiskers' were applied to the nose ends. Incorporated at the apex of the latter was a powerful headlight, a feature aimed at

winning demonstrations overseas. The name *DELTIC* was carried on each side, just below the engine air intakes.

EE was prudent in deciding not to initially ask for the locomotive to be deployed on main-line passenger duties. This was because the machine was complex and might need shake-down

modifications as a result of on-line incidents that could delay a train. Further, coaching stock steam heating boilers were very unreliable, and EE did not want to ruin the locomotive's reputation because of such problems. Instead the company agreed with BR that it should operate main-line freight trains, with Liverpool as its base: the Napier factory in Liverpool had manufactured the engines, while EE's plants at Netherton and Vulcan Foundry, Newton le Willows, were close by. On 28 November 1955 *Deltic* made the first of what became regular runs on the 7.30pm Edge Hill to Camden Town and 7.35pm return the following day. Stabling was at Willesden and Speke Junction between trips.

On 13 December *Deltic* was trialled on its first passenger service, the important 7.10am 'Merseyside Express' from Liverpool Lime Street to London Euston, returning later with the down 'Shamrock Express'. After this solitary exploit, *Deltic* resumed its nocturnal fitted freight diagram. This running experience proved invaluable in improving all aspects of the locomotive. Edge Hill depot provided routine servicing facilities, together with cranage to remove the engine and generator sets. EE always envisaged these being removed for anything beyond minor servicing and designed the locomotive accordingly.

Engine pistons were replaced with a new type that also had less clearance. Such a powerful machine was far from being extended on the duties assigned and the view was formed that it could maintain time with only one engine. To facilitate this, various revisions to the control gear were made. Operating both engines on part load, or idling, for long periods resulted in incomplete combustion. This caused the exhaust emissions to become very smoky, while a build-up of carbon could produce sparks from the exhaust. Tighter pistons were aimed at reducing these emission problems that are one of the downsides of all two-stroke engines.

During August and September 1956

Being built in excess of the standard C1 loading gauge, *Deltic* experienced problems during its trials on the East Coast line because it was too wide for some platforms. On 10 June 1959 it passes Joppa, near Edinburgh.
W. E. Turnbull

Deltic was rigged up and put through a full series of dynamometer car trials over the Settle & Carlisle line. While offering taxing gradients, the overall line speed at the time was only 60mph, thus limiting the extent of high-speed testing. Mobile test cars that could produce varying degrees of rolling resistance were used, rather than traditional coaching stock, although at least one trial was made with a 20-coach train, weighing 642 tons. British Transport Commission Performance and Efficiency Test Bulletin No 19 sets out the findings in great detail.

EE calculated the maximum tractive effort to be 52,500lb and the continuous tractive effort to be 29,000lb at 35mph, making for 2,700hp at the rail (rhp). Whether this was based on the original lower gearing or the revised higher ratio is not known. Concerned about the risk that so powerful a traction unit might cause drawbar failures in its train, especially during surges when wheelslip was encountered, EE had sought to limit maximum tractive effort by causing the main generator to trip out at 2,700A.

At low speed, tractive effort is directly proportional to main generator output. No doubt in conjunction with the BTC, a safe maximum of 48,000lb was settled on when deciding the upper limit of generator current.

During the trials total engine output was calculated to be 3,250bhp, as against 3,300 nominal. This was within normal tolerance. With most diesel-electric designs, rail horsepower (rhp) tends to rise to a peak figure at a speed a little above when the main generator reaches its continuous rating current. Below the continuous rating speed, the generator can operate only for short periods, otherwise it overheats. After that speed, rhp remains fairly constant until main generator unloading occurs. This is the point where rising back electromotive force in the traction motors is not compensated for by rising main generator voltage, and after this speed, rhp declines. With *Deltic*, the measured rhp values were below EE's estimates; this could not be explained by virtue of the difference between the 3,300bhp nominal engine rating and the 3,250bhp measured output for the engines in use in *Deltic*. The following table gives sample values:

Deltic rhp values

Mph	Estimated	Actual	Adjusted
20	2,400	2,380	
30	2,640	2,580	2,620
40	2,777	2,650	2,690
60	2,720	2,650	2,690
80	2,773	2,630	2,670
90	2,640	2,620	2,660

Note: The 'Adjusted' column amends the values in the 'Actual' column to reflect a gross engine output of 3,300bhp, rather than the 3,250bhp developed by the prototype's engines.

EE calculated that generator unloading would occur at 86.5mph, and this reflects in the drop in rhp between 80 and 90mph. In fact, the test results found that this falling away was less pronounced than estimated. Transmission and other losses mean that a diesel-electric (or diesel-hydraulic) cannot deliver full engine output to the bogie wheels; for *Deltic*, the 3,250bhp engine output translated into around 2,650rhp. These losses can be accounted for as follows:

Power absorbed by auxiliary equipment	5%
Power losses in the main generators	6%
Power losses in the traction motors	8%

Subtracting these losses gives a transmission efficiency as 81%, which can be judged to be on the good side. Maximum tractive effort was recorded as 45,500lb, very close to the calculated limit set by EE via the main generator overload trips. This corresponded to only 19% of the locomotive's total weight (or its adhesion factor), which should have meant that *Deltic* was less prone to slipping, because its maximum potential tractive effort was not exploited. Based on the trials, it was calculated that the locomotive would be able to ascend Shap with a 500-ton train at no less than 41mph. During the trials the train was based at Carlisle Durran Hill, the former Midland shed, and some 5,000 miles were run.

During October 1956 *Deltic* was employed mainly on empty stock trains between Edge Hill and Preston, which helped test the train-heating boiler. From the 26th the locomotive was put on to a daily diagram from Lime Street to Euston and return on passenger services. On 31 December this changed to working from Carlisle Upperby shed, from where it made round trips between Carlisle and Euston. After a spell in Netherton Works during the spring of 1957, *Deltic* returned to the Liverpool to London axis until 31 December 1958. To accumulate greater mileages, a fill-in London to Crewe and return duty was added, giving some 700 miles a day.

While the LMR had received the green light for the electrification of the West Coast routes serving Birmingham, Liverpool and Manchester, the ER was sanguine about its chances for the East Coast main line. Its General Manager at the time, Gerard Fiennes, appreciated that the most powerful diesel traction under construction as part of the Modernisation Plan Pilot Scheme would not offer any opportunity for accelerating the route's principal services. He therefore asked for *Deltic* to carry out trials on the East Coast line. Ever a colourful character, Mr Fiennes is said to have described the locomotive as a racehorse, not a giant bullock. This probably represented a side-swipe at the LMR, which had no incentive or desire to deploy it other than on prevailing 8P Pacific turns. Negotiations commenced between BR and EE during 1957 with a view to providing a fleet of 'Deltic' machines for the ER, and there was thus good sense in using the prototype to demonstrate the potential of a 3,300bhp prime mover.

Deltic arrived at Hornsey shed in mid-January 1959. While on the ER, Stratford Works was deputed to carry out maintenance under EE direction. In the flush of enthusiasm to carry out running trials, it is possible that the ER had failed to appreciate that the locomotive had been built to a more generous loading gauge, rather than BR's standard C1.

Above and above right: **After withdrawal,** *Deltic* **was restored cosmetically, but not mechanically, and sent for exhibition at the Science Museum in London. It is seen here carrying a board announcing its presentation to the museum at an unknown location on the newly electrified West Coast route, and in unfamiliar off-rail territory near the museum in Cromwell Road, South Kensington.** *Both EE*

Clearance problems quickly emerged at locations such as Newcastle and York, while it proved necessary to move *Deltic* via the West Coast and Waverley routes to get it to Edinburgh.

As with the LMR, while on the ER a 90mph speed ceiling was imposed, although this was relaxed to 105mph during special tests over certain sections south of Grantham. On 28 February 1960 the 8.20am service from King's Cross, loaded to 250 tons, was taken up Stoke Bank at 100mph. With a 350-ton load, London to Newcastle was run in a time close to that of the inter-war 'Silver Jubilee', although route availability restrictions confined service use to the King's Cross-Doncaster section. This continued until March 1961 when an engine failure saw a return to Vulcan. By

then more than 450,000 miles had been run, and, with the production series locomotives entering traffic, repairs were not deemed worth while.

An enquiry from Canada resulted in a schedule of modifications being drawn up, but the approach came to nothing. *Deltic* languished at Vulcan, gradually being cannibalised for components for the production series, until 28 April 1963, when it was towed by a brand-new EE Type 3 to London for onward road transport to the Science Museum.

Deltic was probably not a commercial success for either EE's Traction Division or Napier, because it only brought two orders, one for 22 similar locomotives for the East Coast route and 10 single-engined locomotives for suburban duties out of King's Cross. It is estimated that

the project cost £400,000. Without DP1 it is highly doubtful whether the BTC would have ordered the production series. However, EE gained valuable experience from the design and construction work, which must have been of help with later projects. Problems encountered with *Deltic* brought changes to aspects of the production series design. Napier made modifications to the engines, notably to the injectors and exhaust system, which brought a redesignation to D18-25A. EE produced a revised main generator and traction motors because those in the prototype had not proved as reliable as desired. Overall, *Deltic* must be judged as having fulfilled its purpose satisfactorily, without being a resounding success.

Deltic

Length	67ft 9in
Width	8ft 9½in
Height	12ft 10in
Weight	106 tons
Wheel diameter	3ft 7in
Engines	2 x Napier Deltic D18-11B
Engine output	1,650bhp at 1,500rpm
Max speed	105mph
Tractive effort (revised gearing), maximum	48,000lb
continuous	23,400lb at 43.5mph
Gear ratio, original	61:19
revised	59:21
Fuel tank capacity	800 gallons
Minimum curve radius	6 chains

EE Rotation Number 2007 of 1954

Pilot Scheme Prototypes of Type A

The Modernisation Plan

In 1955 the Government sanctioned the Modernisation Plan to combat the worsening financial situation on Britain's railways. It encompassed investment in new track and signalling, major station upgrading, new rolling stock and major construction of marshalling yard facilities. Work on the Plan started well before its authorisation, and on 6 October 1954 a proposal was unveiled for the order of 171 diesel locomotives for evaluation; this was later increased by three. It was not, however, until 16 November 1955 that orders were actually placed for what became known as the Pilot Scheme.

Details of the locomotives ordered are set out in the following table and will be described in this and the following two chapters, split between the original classification of Type A (800 to 1,000hp), Type B (1,000 to 1,500hp) and Type C (2,000 to 2,500hp) machines.

The plan was that these prototypes would be evaluated over a three-year period to enable sensible decisions to be taken as to which should be multiplied in squadron production, a highly sensible approach. However, this was not fulfilled because in September 1956 the BTC ordered a further 28 NBL Class 21s, 10 BR Class 24s and 18 BRCW Class 26s,

Bhp	TOPS Class	Number series	Main contractor	Engine type	Number
Class A					
800	15	D8200-9	BTH	Paxman 16YHXL	10
800	16	D8400-9	NBL	Paxman 16YHXL	10
1,000	20	D8000-19	EE	EE 8SVT Mk II	20
Class B					
1,000	21	D6100-9	NBL	MAN L12V18/21	10
1,000	22	D6300-5	NBL	MAN L12V18/21	6
1,100	23	D5900-9	EE	Napier T9-29	10
1,160	24	D5000-19	BR	Sulzer 6LDA28A	20
1,160	26	D5300-19	BRCW	Sulzer 6LDA28A	20
1,200	28	D5700-19	Metro-Vick	Crossley HSTV8	20
1,250	30	D5500-19	Brush	Mirrlees JVS12T	20
Class C					
2,000	40	D200-9	EE	EE 16SVT Mk II	10
2,000	41	D600-4	NBL	MAN L12V18/21	5
2,000	42	D800-2	BR	Maybach MD650	3
2,300	44	D1-10	BR	Sulzer 12LDA28A	10
				Total	**174**

Classes 22, 41 and 42 were diesel-hydraulic, the remainder being diesel-electric. Class 42 was actually not ordered until February 1956.

This view of BTH Type 1 No D8200 was taken while the locomotive was still in primer, and sees it during trials over the Settle & Carlisle line at Settle in November 1957. *Ian Allan Library*

while during February 1957 a further 115 diesel-hydraulics for the WR were sanctioned. In July 1956 BR changed its motive power classifications from letters to numbers, from 1 to 5, Classes A and B becoming Types 1 and 2 respectively. The previous gap between 1,500 and 2,000hp now became Type 3, and the old Class C was now Type 4. The remainder of this chapter now considers the Class A or Type 1 Pilot Scheme prototypes.

BTH D8200 series
(later Class 15)

While BTH was the main contractor, three other companies played a significant part in producing this class, more than for any other type. Construction of the mechanical parts was, unusually, split between the Clayton Equipment Company Ltd and Yorkshire Engine Co Ltd: the former built the bogies and superstructure, while the latter built the frames and undertook the final assembly. Paxman supplied the diesel and BTH the electrical equipment. The cost price was £56,485.

The general arrangement of the design followed that of No 10800 in that the single cab was located between the power plant and cooler group at one end and the control cubicle at the other. Although the BTC did not specify a train-heating capability, a through pipe was provided to enable a pilot locomotive to provide steam for train-heating purposes. Access to components was made easy by provision of full-height doors along the bodyside, together with removable roof compartments. Unusually, engine room air was drawn in through louvres at cantrail level without being filtered. Air maze filters were, though, provided for generator, compressor and traction motor air.

The cooler group was located in the nose end, with the radiator fan driven by a shaft from the free end of the engine. The driver could vary the air supply to the radiators by changing the position of the side-panel louvres, which were air-operated, a novel feature. A 16-cylinder Paxman YHXL diesel, rated at 800bhp at 1,250rpm, was used, the rating being 200bhp lower than the manufacturer's continuous figure. Coupled to the engine was a 6-pole BTH RTB 10858 main generator, rated at 500kW, 690/337V, 720/1320A at 1,250rpm. Overhung from

Top: **The finished product: No D8201 poses for the official photograph.** *Ian Allan Library*

Above: **Initially based at the former North London Railway depot at Devons Road, No D8201 is recorded at Kensal Green Junction on a transfer freight.** *Ian Allan Library*

the end of the main generator was an RTB 7420 40kW auxiliary alternator. Unusually, there was a separate differential exciter (model DY2816) for the main generator, which was belt-driven from the latter and mounted on top of the auxiliary generator. All the above was housed in the main bonnet end of the locomotive.

Four BTH 137AZ traction motors continuously rated at 144hp, 380V, 330A at 375rpm, were mounted one per axle in the usual nose-suspended arrangement. Connected in parallel on Bo-Bo bogies, one stage of field weakening was used. The control scheme was designed to prevent overloading the motors with current while the locomotive was stationary. This was achieved by combining the demands from the driver's power controller and the automatic load control. In line with the envisaged operating routine, the locomotive's top speed was 60mph.

On 23 October 1957 No D8200 made a trial run from Yorkshire Engineering Company's Meadowhall (Sheffield) works to Chinley, hauling one coach. During early November some initial testing had already been carried out over the Settle & Carlisle line, at which time the locomotive was still in grey primer — the final livery was green. The locomotive was handed over to BR at a ceremony at Euston station on 18 November 1957, and later that day was observed at Hayden Square Yard in East London, where it replaced a D8000 series engine. Seemingly intended for deployment in East Anglia as part of the plan for rapid elimination of steam, this was changed and allocation was to

the new diesel shed at Devons Road, Bow, an LMR establishment despite its location in East London. A former North London Railway facility, the switch seems to owe something to the 1956 Clean Air Act and the City of London's desire to eradicate pollution caused by steam engines.

Thus the D8200 series locomotives first found employment on cross-London freights between Poplar, Temple Mills, Willesden and Acton yards, pretty much the type of work for which they had been conceived. During April 1958 the LMR carried out trials with Nos D8202/4 in multiple on the West Coast line as possible substitutes for pairs of D8000s. There was a hiccup in deliveries due to a strike in the manufacturer's works during the month. Nos D8203/8 spent some time during November 1958 at Toton for crew training, then a month later the latter migrated to Scotland for evaluation at Polmadie, Thornton Junction and Kittybrewster,

Longer-distance freights were often operated by two Type 1s in multiple, as seen here, with No D8202 leading.
Railway Industry Association

When transferred to the ER most of the class spent their time allocated to Stratford. Local parcels turns were regularly entrusted to the BTH Type 1s, and No D8208 sits at Liverpool Street on 21 January 1961. *M. Mensing*

returning south hauling a Waverley Route freight. Back in East London, as soon as sufficient D8000s had been built the LMR happily palmed off the D8200s to the ER for their initially intended utilisation on the Great Eastern Section. During 1958 the class averaged only 16,842 miles, while when transferred to the ER this rose to 25,606 and availability that year was creditable at 83%.

The class spread its wings as later builds outside the Pilot Scheme arrived, and could be found across the whole of East Anglia, handling local passenger traffic in the summer, serving as station pilots, and working parcels and freight trains. The 1960s found the class still pottering around East Anglia, primarily on freight services that were light enough to be covered by a single locomotive, although having the BR Blue Star coupling code meant that they could work in multiple with most diesel classes. However, road competition was making vast inroads into the volume of this traffic, and redundancy thus loomed for the BTH Type 1s.

For such a small engine, the Paxman diesel, arguably, had too many cylinders — 16 — which multiplied maintenance time and problems with component failures. Unfortunately that was not the only issue faced by depots. Piston seizures were addressed by retro-fitting oil-cooled pistons, together with wider piston rings. The use of an aluminium sleeve for the injectors proved inadequate and allowed water into the cylinders, causing connecting rod failure, so steel sleeves were fitted instead. Soon after this modification, the cylinder heads began to crack and let water and oil into the cylinder with the same result as before. It took two attempts with modified heads to cure the problem.

Carbon built up on the turbocharger gas entry ports, mainly due to the diesel spending long periods idling or on low power, a feature of the locomotive's operating regime. A related issue was an inadequate charge being put into the batteries, again stemming from the operating regime. Fitting larger-diameter drain pipes in the turbochargers made

them less prone to blockage and helped reduce the carbon build-up. An Ardleigh engine governor was used for the first time in Britain in this class; this used unfiltered engine oil, resulting in dirt clogging the mechanism and causing erratic performance of the component and, consequentially, the engine. Fitting oil filters cured the problem. Oil leaking from the cylinders could find its way on to the exhaust system lagging, and a fire was the inevitable result.

The electrical machines appear to have worked well, although problems did arise with the control equipment. An order for a further 34 machines came very quickly, with construction this time being handled by Clayton entirely at its Derby Works. These benefited from some of the modifications found necessary and described above. Nevertheless, overall, the BTH Class A/Type 1 was not a conspicuous success. It was relatively expensive to keep running and always had to be doubled-manned on the footplate because of visibility issues when working long-bonnet-leading. Under the 1967 National Traction Plan the class was deemed non-standard and expendable, resulting in most being withdrawn by 1970 and the remainder by March 1971. None of the Pilot Scheme batch survive.

Without train-heating equipment, all the Type 1s were restricted to working passenger trains during the summer. No D8202 heads for Yarmouth Vauxhall in July 1960 with a special from Derby.
John C. Baker

D8200 series	
Length	42ft 3³/₈ in
Width	9ft 2in
Height	12ft 6in
Weight	68 tons
Wheel diameter	3ft 3½in
Engine	Paxman 16YHXL
Engine output	800bhp
Maximum speed	60mph
Tractive effort,	
maximum	40,000lb
continuous	19,700lb at 11.3mph
Gear ratio	65:16
Fuel tank capacity	400 gallons
Minimum curve radius	3½ chains

BTH Works Numbers 1031-1040 and Clayton Equipment Co Works Numbers CE3519/1-10

NBL D8400 series
(later Class 16)

Very little has been written about this ill-starred design. Externally it resembled the BTH D8200s and, of course, the NBL prototype, No 10800. Internally it shared the same Paxman engine as the D8200 class, but NBL opted to link up with GEC for the electrical machines. A GEC WT881 6-pole main generator continuously rated at 505kW, 1,700A, 290V at 1,250rpm, and a GEC WT761 35kW auxiliary generator were used, together with four GEC WT 441 traction motors continuously rated at 152hp at 420rpm, taking 435A at 300V. The internal layout also copied that of No 10800. Construction took place at NBL's Hyde Park Works, one of its three production facilities in Glasgow, under NBL Order HP 78. Assigned running numbers D8400-9, the livery was green with a light grey roof and duck-egg-blue cab doors. No D8400 was completed in July 1958 and, after initial testing around Glasgow, was sent to Stratford, eventually the home of the whole class. The final construction cost was £58,133.

Obviously the same problems with the Paxman engines affected the type as already described above. Additionally, though, NBL's seeming inability to design an effective engine cooling system led also to engine seizures, a major defect causing locomotives to be sidelined for long periods on occasions. A further downside was NBL's adoption of electric, rather than pneumatic, engine control. It was not unique in this decision, and it can be argued that the system is more reliable, while drivers do not really need the infinitely variable control of power that the pneumatic system offers. Nevertheless, the upshot was a Red Circle coupling code that precluded working in multiple with the BTH equivalents.

The first reported sighting of the class involved No D8400 at Doncaster Works on 2 June 1958 with a five-coach test train bound for Barkston, near Grantham. Clearly all was not well, because on 15 July both Nos D8400/1 were sent back to NBL for attention, while the next day No D8402 was noted heading south through Edinburgh, followed two days

Above left: **Class doyen No D8400 during its first reported sighting on 2 June 1958, at Doncaster Works for acceptance tests. Note the lack of livery embellishment.** *P. Tait*

Left: **Throughout their lives all the NBL Type 1s were allocated to Stratford, where No D8400 is seen during 1961.** *Ian Allan Library*

Above: **A rare photo of NBL Types 1 and 2 together. With an EE Type 4 behind, No D8401 is stabled with Type 2 No D6114, possibly at Stratford.** *R. C. Riley*

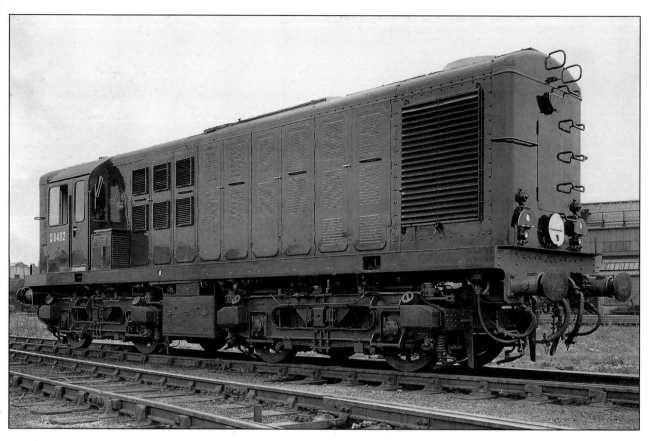

later by No D8403. On 7 August Nos D8402/3 were noted on test on the Southend Victoria line. In September Nos D8400/1 were still, seemingly, undergoing tests from Doncaster when sighted at Newark Northgate, and on the 21st Nos D8400-5 were dumped on Stratford depot due to overheating problems.

On 19 November No D8400 was seen heading for the SR with a freight via the Snow Hill line. Displacement of LNER 'J11' steam power continued with No D8407 noted on 14 January 1959 traversing London Transport's Epping line with a short goods train. During the following summer the class was entrusted with holiday passenger duties in the East London area to Southend Victoria. Visits to Stratford Works during the latter part of the year invariably found at least two examples out of the 10 under repair.

The history of the class then mirrors that of the BTH Type 1s, and the two classes seem to have been used turn-and-turn-about by Stratford depot. With the planned work dying out, it was no

Above left: **This fine study of No D8402 shows its features clearly, including the handle used by the driver to open and close the radiator shutters.** *Ian Allan Library*

Above: **No caption information is available for this view of an NBL Type 1, but note that it has acquired a silver or grey roof.** *Ian Allan Library*

Left: **Another livery variation, this time to aid visibility for permanent way staff, was painting the cab doors yellow. A rare passenger outing over SR metals occurred on 22 May 1960 when No D8408 worked a Leyton to Brighton special, seen crossing the Ouse Viaduct.** *Stanley Creer*

Another livery variation was a yellow panel on the locomotive ends. This example is said to be heading for Epping to shunt the yard. *J. K. Carter*

surprise that the class found no place in the National Traction Plan and the entire fleet was withdrawn by the end of 1968.

D8400 series

Length	42ft 6in
Width	8ft 8½in
Height	12ft 8in
Weight	68 tons
Wheel diameter	3ft 7in
Engine	Paxman 16YHXL
Engine output	800bhp
Maximum speed	60mph
Tractive effort, maximum	42,000lb
continuous	20,000lb at 10.8mph
Gear ratio	71:15
Fuel tank capacity	490 gallons
Minimum curve radius	3½ chains

NBL Progressive Numbers 27671-27680

EE D8000 series (later Class 20)

The final Class A order went to EE (Contract Number CCF 0873 and BR Lot Number 256 of 1957) for 20 locomotives at a price of £58,955 using an eight-cylinder version of the EE SVT Mark 2 diesel, here rated at 1,000bhp at 850rpm, that had been installed in No 10203. Electrical equipment and the engine came from EE, with the mechanical portion and assembly contracted to Vulcan Foundry, recently absorbed into EE. Unlike the other two designs, this Bo-Bo had its single cab at one end of the hood. The basic equipment arrangement did, though, mirror the other designs by having the cooler group in the nose, then the engine and generator set, with the control cubicle at the other end of the hood, adjoining the cab; this enabled access to the cubicle from the cab. The bonnet superstructure had opening hatches in the sides and removable roof panels to provide access during maintenance.

EE's Preston site built the engines. A shaft from one end of the engine turned the radiator fan, with the opening of the radiator shutters being under driver control. The EE 819/3C main generator was attached to the diesel and was continuously rated at 642kW, 1,070A, 600V at 850rpm. The EE911/2B 48kW auxiliary generator was mounted above at the former's free end. The four EE 526/5D traction motors were continuously rated at 212hp at 362rpm, 600A at a nominal 300V; connected in series-parallel and nose-suspended, one per bogie axle, they were geared for a 75mph locomotive top speed. A green livery with light grey roof was applied.

No D8000 was the first Pilot Scheme locomotive to enter traffic. It arrived at Willesden on 18 June 1957 and was officially allocated to its home shed of Devons Road four days later. The order

was fulfilled with the arrival of No D8019 at Devons Road on 4 March 1958. Here they were used indiscriminately with the other Type 1s, but their better turn of speed allowed deployment during the summer months on passenger services. In 1959 they averaged 24,917 miles. Devons Road closed in February 1964 and Nos D8000-12 moved elsewhere on the LMR, while D8013-19 became ER property.

Initial service experience showed up only two problems. The original engine camshafts had been manufactured too soft and had to be replaced. Poor instrumentation led to incorrect calibration of the engine fuel pumps, causing some cylinders to be devoid of fuel when the engine was idling; unburnt engine oil was therefore discharged through the exhaust stacks. Better calibration methods solved the problem. Otherwise the EE Type 1 proved to be an excellent design, easily the best among the Pilot Scheme orders.

It quickly fell from favour, though, due

Immaculate for its official picture, EE Type 1 No D8000 stands at the rear of Vulcan Foundry in June 1957. Note the silver paint used to relieve the green livery, together with the white tyre faces. *EE*

Top: New locomotives were sent from Liverpool Edge Hill Carriage Sidings to Penrith as part of their trial programme. No D8000 is recorded near Oxenholme during its trial on 17 June 1957. *W. Hubert Foster*

Above: An official photograph of the same trial, taken during a station stop in the northern fells on the northbound run. *EE*

Top: **This undated official LMR photograph of a pair of EE Type 1s, with No D8002 leading, gives the train as the 10pm Broad Street to Carlisle, which is interesting because it was quite clearly taken during daylight hours!** *LMR*

Above: **Another pair of EE Type 1s, Nos D8000/45, head up the West Coast line at South Kenton in July 1958.** *Derek Cross*

Top: The first allocation for all the Pilot Scheme order was Devons Road in East London. Before the new diesel depot there opened, No D8003 shares the steam shed facilities with 'Jinties' Nos 47483 and 47560 on 31 August 1957. *Brian Morrison*

Above: The EE Type 1s also had duties out of London Euston. No D8001 shunts parcels vans in the terminus on 21 October 1961. *M. Mensing*

Above: EE Type 1s also found use on outer London diagrams. On 31 August 1964 No D8003 descends towards Euston with the 7.30 from Tring. *Brian Stephenson*

Left: What the photographer claims to be the inaugural visit of the class to Brighton sees No D8014 there on 15 January 1958. *W. M. J. Jackson*

to the single-cab bonnet design that enforced double-manning to ensure visibility, unless operating in multiple. While additional orders were forthcoming, in 1960 BR announced a new centre-cab Type 1 (later Class 17). That the Paxman engines fitted in the new standard proved troublesome falls outside the scope of this book, but when BR later required additional Type 1s, it again fell back on the proven EE class and the numbers finally totalled 228 by 1968. When the National Traction Plan discarded all the other Type 1 classes, only Class 20 survived. By then almost always working in pairs, their reliability and availability figures ensured longevity, while low gearing enabled utilisation on 45-wagon 'merry-go-round' (MGR) coal trains of 2,000 tons on the LMR. Allocations were on all Regions bar the Western, though the class made daily visits on freight and occasional trips as far as Cornwall on weed-killing trains. Representatives of the class remain in use, including, from the Pilot Scheme batch, No D8001 in preservation and Nos D8007/16 with RFS. Class doyen No D8000, later No 20050, was withdrawn in December 1980 but was restored as part of the National Collection.

D8000 series	
Length	46ft 9³⁄₈in
Width	8ft 9in
Height	12ft 7⁵⁄₈in
Weight	72 tons
Wheel diameter	3ft 7in
Engine	EE 8SVT Mk II
Engine output	1,000bhp
Maximum speed	75mph
Tractive effort,	
maximum	42,000lb
continuous	19,500lb at 14.8mph
Gear ratio	63:17
Fuel tank capacity	400 gallons
Minimum curve radius	3½ chains

EE Rotation Numbers 2347-2366 and Vulcan Foundry Works Numbers D375-D394

Above: **In the 1960s the Pilot Scheme locomotives spread far and wide. On 16 May 1978 Nos 20002/149 visit Crianlarich as part of a through freight working from Fort William to the Glasgow area.**
Tom Heavyside

Left: **Borrowed from 'merry-go-round' work off Springs Branch, Nos 20016/001 find employment on Sunday West Coast diversions at the head of the 08.50 Crewe to Blackpool North train on 30 June 1985. It is seen here at Lostock Junction where the train will reverse direction and take the route on the right of the picture.**
Tom Heavyside

NBL D6100 and D6300 series
(later Classes 21 and 22)

Whereas the Type A designs were specified by the BTC to have a single cab and no train heating, Type B was to have a cab at each end, a Bo-Bo axle configuration, a top speed of 75mph and a steam generator. As with the smaller Type 1s, equipment to permit multiple working was to be included, and the maximum axle load was not to exceed 18¾ tons. Duties to be covered were to comprise suburban passenger and a range of freight services, with two or more operating in multiple on Class 1 express passenger or heavy freight, if necessary.

These two classes comprised 10 and six examples respectively and were similar,

apart from the former having electric transmission, while the latter had a hydraulic drive and were specifically for the WR. NBL had acquired UK licences for MAN engines and offered the L12V18/21A model, a 12-cylinder, four-stroke unit, with a rating of 1,000bhp at 1,500rpm in Class 21 and 1,445rpm in Class 22. Subsequent production series orders had a revised rating of 1,100bhp at 1,500rpm for Class 21 and at 1530rpm for Class 22. While Paxman's RPH diesel had been installed in prototype No 10800 and Paxman was supplying its YHXL 16-cylinder diesel for the NBL Type A (later Class 16), NBL offered the MAN design in its tender to the BTC for a Type B locomotive. Nothing has come to light to suggest the company had manufactured

No D6112 stands at Doncaster on 25 May 1959, brand-new and awaiting commissioning.
Brian Morrison

An official publicity view of the NBL Type 2, taken at Royston. Note that only very limited embellishment was applied to No D6100's BR green livery. *British Railways*

previously this German design and, indeed, this could well have been the Glasgow company's first experience in engine manufacture.

In the design of No 10800, NBL had teamed up with BTH for the electrical machines, but the latter had since forged alliances with other builders as part of the Pilot Scheme bidding process, so GEC was approached instead. It supplied its 6-pole WT 880 main generator with duplex lap winding, continuously rated at 637.5 kW, 1,700A, 375V at 1,500rpm, together with the WT761 35kW, 318A, 110V auxiliary generator and four WT 440 traction motors, continuously rated at 189rhp, 425A, 375V at 372rpm. Designed for a top speed of 75mph, the gearing reflected the required performance characteristic with a continuous rating speed of 11mph and full power available between 4.3 and 75mph. Maximum tractive effort was given as 45,000lb, while the continuous tractive effort was calculated as 25,000lb, offering 733hp at the rail.

Almost by way of a sop to the WR's lobbying for a trial of diesel-hydraulic drive, the BTC agreed to place an order with NBL for a hydraulic version of its diesel-electric Type B, together with a Type C, which will be described in the next chapter. Hence the principal difference came in the transmission, with a Voith L306r turbo-transmission used. In choosing a single locomotive design from the same builder, the BTC would be able to compare closely the two forms of propulsion. NBL had also acquired manufacturing rights from Voith and, again, this seems to have been the first experience the company had of manufacturing the components. Substitution of the different transmission gave a slightly different performance characteristic. According to the BR Diagram Book, the maximum tractive effort was 41,920lb at 27.6% adhesion factor, and the continuous tractive effort was 23,900lb at 10.4mph. Overall weight was slightly lighter at 67 tons 16cwt.

The body had a neat appearance, with

Top left: **The Pilot Scheme NBL Type 2 diesel-electrics were destined for suburban duties out of King's Cross. No D6108 passes Potters Bar during May 1959 with an up Cambridge Buffet Car express.** *Ian Allan Library*

Left: **After migrating to Glasgow during April 1960, ostensibly to be close to NBL's works for rectification, the class worked far and wide. This picture is particularly interesting because it shows the retention of pre-nationalisation service patterns– the train comprises combined portions from the ex-LMS stations of Glasgow Buchanan Street and Edinburgh Princes Street, and is bound for Oban via the Callander route. Nos D6102 and D6123 descend the 1 in 50 from Glencruitten Crossing on the final run into Oban on 16 May 1961.** *M. Mensing*

Top: **Although Class 5 steam power had previously been used on the 10.15am 'Granite City' Glasgow Buchanan Street to Aberdeen service, the ScR deployed two NBL Type 2s. Nos D6103 and 6100 prepare to leave Stonehaven on 18 August 1962.** *W. A. C. Smith*

Above: **Roughly half the Pilot Scheme batch were selected to receive a Paxman engine with a view to raising reliability. The converts became Class 29 and acquired front-end headcode panels, as demonstrated in this view of No D6101.** *N. E. Preedy*

The diesel-hydraulic version of the NBL Type 2 was to be deployed initially west of Newton Abbot as part of the elimination of steam. In this September 1959 view, No D6309 pilots 'Castle' class No 5054 *Earl of Ducie* on a Manchester to Penzance train at Aller Junction. *Derek Cross*

two curving cab windows atop nose-end gangway doors. BR green livery was applied, with a horizontal light grey line at solebar level between the cab doors. The numbers D6100-9 were given to the diesel-electric type and D6300-5 to the diesel-hydraulic version. Following NBL practice in the use of electric power control, the D6100s had the Red Circle multiple coupling code, though some of the later production series had pneumatic control and thus were of the Blue Star type. Nos D6300-5, however, had electro-pneumatic control and were classed as Orange Square, but the later series adopted NBL's electric engine control and were White Diamond in consequence. All of the Type 4 'Warships' (see Chapter 5), apart from the Pilot Scheme designs, had the latter coupling code. NBL's original quotes for the two designs were £62,400 and £53,000, while the final prices were £69,853 and £63,953 respectively. During 1957 both variants of the locomotive were re-ordered by the BTC and incorporated

some detail differences from their respective prototypes.

It had been intended that the D6100s would go to the ER, and the Pilot Scheme batch went new to Hornsey depot on the former Great Northern line, to carry out a mix of local passenger, freight and empty stock movements. Within a short time of being placed into traffic, in November 1959 the BTC resolved to eliminate the NBL Type 2 diesel-electrics, such were their deficiencies. The later builds were assigned to Stratford for Great Eastern Line tasks, similar to those of Hornsey's allocation.

No D6300 was noted passing Lenzie on the Glasgow to Edinburgh line on 2 December 1958, no doubt under test. Working off Doncaster, BR conducted acceptance trials along the East Coast as far as Grantham and Peterborough, No D6100 being observed at Newark on 5, 8, 12 and 13 December. Clearly there were problems because Nos D6100/4 did not arrive at Hornsey until 2 March 1959,

In this attractive scene, taken on Dainton bank on 22 August 1959, No D6301's clear exhaust belies the hard effort as it assists 'Hall' class No 4931 *Hanbury Hall*, which was deputising for a larger class of steam traction, on the 11.00am Paddington to Penzance service. *J. R. Ainslie*

while Nos D6101/2 were sent back to their makers. Although No D6109 had reached Hornsey by 14 April, Nos D6104/5/7/9 had been returned to Doncaster Works.

Naturally the No D6300s were destined for the WR and were to feature prominently in eliminating steam in the West Country. Although this was the case for all Class 22s, the Pilot Scheme six were largely confined to South Devon and Cornwall because of their incompatibility for multiple-unit working with later No D6300s; this was because the Pilot Scheme batch was designed to multiple with the NBL D600s (see Chapter 5). All the class were to be used on freight and secondary passenger duties west and north of Exeter, as well as serving as pilots over the South Devon banks.

No D6300 arrived at Swindon in mid-December 1958 and entered traffic on 12 January 1959, based at Plymouth Laira, with deliveries to the same shed up to No D6304 by 23 June. For some reason No D6305 did not enter service until 11 January 1960, later than the first two of the production series, although it had been delivered during the summer of 1959. No D6300 spent three weeks from 14 January 1959 primarily on the 7.55am Swindon to Bath local passenger, and this area of operation was used for the assessment of all new deliveries. Once in service, deployment was on a wide range of local passenger and freight across the West Country, as well as use in pairs on expresses, including the SR route between Plymouth and Exeter Central. The class also acted as pilots between Newton Abbot and Plymouth.

As service experience was gained, so the problems with both types grew. All the No D6300s are reputed to have been sent back to NBL during the spring of 1959 for modification, while by August 1959 Hornsey's stud was achieving only 51% availability. NBL had as much experience of diesel locomotive design and

Newton Abbot was where the pilot locomotive was attached for the assault of the severe climbs onwards to Plymouth. In July 1959 No D6301 assists 'Castle' class No 5028 *Llantilio Castle* with the down 'Cornish Riviera Express' as they restart the train. *D S. Fish*

construction as any other company, and more than most in Britain, at the time the Pilot Scheme orders were placed, but despite this, its products for BR proved to be the worst of all the orders. This has been attributed to an inability to make a successful transition from the heavy engineering standards required for steam traction to the greater precision involved with diesels.

There were detail shortcomings in all the NBL designs, notably engine cooling systems. Component positioning within the locomotive meant that simple, minor faults could be resolved only in a depot or works, cutting down availability for traffic. Manufacturing of the engines was not to the appropriate tolerances, or with

proper finishing-off. The engines leaked, the cylinder heads failed, and oil seeped into the battery box, among other issues. Problems arose with the coupling arrangement between the engine and main generator. The GEC electrical machines seem to have added to the troubles, with some main generators burning out, while engine room fires were common and caused several D6100s to be withdrawn.

NBL technicians spent much time at St Rollox Works attending to faults, but this ceased in 1962 when the company closed due to insolvency. For some time prior to this event, strong political pressure had been applied for extra work to keep the Glasgow works operating. Such was the

No doubt after receiving attention at Swindon Works, Nos D6301 and D6302 head a test train past Tuffley Junction, Gloucester, amid the snow of 15 January 1959.
P. J. Sharpe

disastrous reputation of all the works' output that the BTC refused to relent and, with no new business, NBL failed. This then added to the problems of those looking after its locomotives because the existing slow supply of spares became exacerbated.

Again, the company's failure to grasp key elements of diesel construction seems to have been a factor, because Swindon reported in 1962 that all the MAN engines were non-standard, ie of inconsistent construction. This report identified 17 major problem areas with the engines alone, and, of course, these problems were common to all NBL's MAN units. It has been said that the MAN engine design was not as good as Maybach's, and had

been hurriedly conceived to get a toe-hold in the German rail market at the time of the V200 locomotive order. In truth, the MAN engines were not selected for squadron use in these locomotives because they did not prove to be as good as the Maybach equivalent. Swindon also identified five defects with the Voith transmission, although, overall, it was satisfactory.

Chronic unreliability must have been experienced because by March 1960 Hornsey's fleet moved to New England Yard at Peterborough for store. Possibly while there they were spotted sheeted over and the *Daily Telegraph* reported that new diesels were being dumped and hidden away — questions were then

Above: An interesting study at a familiar location, Penzance, on 12 May 1959. Two of the Pilot Scheme Type 2s, Nos D6300 and D6302, have been rostered for the 'Royal Duchy' to Paddington. It is likely that the pair would be replaced at Plymouth. *A. Robey*

Right: By the time this undated view of No D6302 was taken, train headcode boxes and a half-height warning panel had been added to the nose ends. *A. Swain*

asked in Parliament! These problems may have been a factor in the decision to move all the No D6100s to Scotland, supposedly so that they could be near NBL's works for repair, but allegedly to get them away from the eyes of those with a voice. Locos seem to have migrated north in pairs during mid-April 1960. The WR, meanwhile, had to continue to suffer with the D6300s.

In an attempt to resolve persistent problems with the MAN engines, in 1963 one of the production series D6100s, No D6123, was fitted with a Paxman 12YJXL 'Ventura' diesel, of the type that had been trialled in BR/Swindon Type 4 No D830 in place of the Maybach MD650 engine (see Chapter 9). This change proved reasonably successful to the point where a further 19 locomotives were converted between 1965 and 1967 by BR at its St Rollox, Glasgow and Inverurie Works, and among the prototype batch, Nos D6100-3/6-8 were selected for conversion, No D6100 being one of the last in December 1967. At least one had been in store as unserviceable for more than four years.

Rated at 1,350bhp, the rebuilds were redesignated as Class 29. After a spell on the West Highland lines, the converts were displaced for a second time by the more reliable BRCW/Sulzer Type 2s (later Class 27). Nevertheless, when candidates were being considered for weeding out as part of the 1967 National Traction Plan, it was no surprise when all the NBL Type 2s were selected for withdrawal. Most of the Class 21s were withdrawn in 1967 and only Class 29 survived to 1971, with four of the Pilot Scheme batch lasting until October of that year. On the WR Nos D6300-5 had been confined to South Devon and Cornwall by virtue of being non-standard with other No D6300s. This helped in the decision to withdraw them first when traffic levels fell, and branch lines were closed and they became surplus. Apart from No D6301, which succumbed on 30 December 1967, the remainder bowed out on 26 May 1968.

None of the NBL Type 2s survive.

NBL Type 2s

	Class 21	Class 22
Length	51ft 6in	46ft 8½in
Width	8ft 8in	8ft 8in
Height	12ft 8in	12ft 10in
Weight	72 tons 10cwt	67 tons 16cwt
Wheel diameter	3ft 7in	3ft 7in
Engine	MAN L12V18/21BS	MAN L12V18/21BS
Engine output	1,000bhp at 1,500rpm	1,000bhp at 1,445rpm
Maximum speed	75mph	75mph
Tractive effort, maximum	45,000lb	41,920lb
continuous	25,000lb at 11mph	23,900lb at 10.4mph
Gear ratio	64:15	-
Fuel tank capacity	460 gallons	450 gallons
Minimum curve radius	4½ chains	4½ chains

Note: The engine code in German was L12V18/21A.
D6100-9 carried North British Locomotive Co Progressive Numbers 27681-90.
Construction was under NBL Locomotive Order HP (Hyde Park Works) 79.
D6300-5 carried North British Locomotive Co Progressive Numbers 27665-70.
Construction was under NBL Locomotive Order QP (Queens Park) 77.
BR Swindon Lot No 426 was also issued.

EE D5900 'Baby Deltic' series (later Class 23)

Considering that this was a Pilot Scheme order, it seems that EE did not actually place an internal order for construction until 23 January 1957 (Contract CCF 0875), with the mechanical parts and assembly being handled by Vulcan Foundry. This, no doubt, came after the design details had been worked out. The contract price with BR was £71,400, but the price paid was £79,110. As with the D6100s, the design had to take account of a requirement to work from King's Cross over the Metropolitan Widened Lines to Moorgate.

A conventional strength underframe was used to provide the main load-bearing support for the body, with external styling similar to the EE Type C, also ordered under the Pilot Scheme, and it incorporated a pronounced nose end. The bogies were similar to those being fitted to the EE Type A Pilot Scheme order. A nine-cylinder Napier Deltic T9-29 1,100bhp turbocharged engine was used, coupled to which was an EE six-pole Type 835/7A or 8D main

generator continuously rated at 680kW, 1,700A, 400V at 1,600rpm, and a 4-pole EE Type 912/1B 45kW, 410A, 110V at 1,000/2,680rpm auxiliary generator. Although use of the same EE526 traction motor as that in both the EE Type A and C locomotives would have offered savings on stock holding, the company agreed a change with the BTC to bring down the continuous rating speed. Thus four EE533A 6-pole motors were fitted, continuously rated at 250hp, 850A, 250V at 350rpm, giving a continuous rating speed of 9.4mph, rather than 14.8mph in the Type A locomotive. The traction motor 1-hour rating was 264hp, 900A, 250V at 340rpm. Standard BR green was used for the body, with a light grey band at solebar level, changing to red around the nose ends. The roof was to be mid-grey, with black for the undergear and bogies. Running numbers D5900-9 were assigned.

As built No D5900 was 3 tons overweight at 75 tons. This was unacceptable to BR, and had arisen mainly because the mechanical parts had been beefed up to compensate for the lower weight of the engine. Much thought was given to this, and it was eventually reduced to a service weight of 73 tons 17cwt. Dealing with the weight problem caused No D5902 to be the first to undertake the customary (for a Vulcan-built machine) trial from Vulcan to Chester to check instrumentation and fitness to run. This was on 1 April 1959, followed on the 3rd by a loaded trial between Edge Hill and Penrith. Doncaster Works then carried out acceptance testing.

Left: **Brand-new and positively gleaming, on 25 May 1959 No D5901 awaits commissioning at Doncaster Works.** *Brian Morrison*

Below left: **This official photograph of No D5908 has been included because it shows off clearly the unusual feature of a nose-end ladder.** *EE*

Below: **The EE Type 2 'Baby Deltics' were intended for outer suburban diagrams from King's Cross. No D5907 passes Hadleigh Wood during July 1959 with a down Peterborough train.** *Derek Cross*

Planned use was on the ER Great Northern Section, and the class appeared at Hornsey depot between April and June, moving to Finsbury Park when that depot opened. Here they were deployed on outer-suburban passenger turns from King's Cross to Hitchin and Cambridge, as well as some freight activity. Initial experience was poor, due to power unit and auxiliary equipment failures, most of the latter components coming from specialist suppliers and not fit for the purpose. Bearing in mind that the ER had ordered 22 production Type 5 versions of the prototype 'Deltic', there must have been worries all round at the D5900 series reliability. By October 1960 44 engine changes across the fleet of 10 locomotives had occurred, and the problems multiplied with cooling system defects, among others.

Napier undertook to rebuild the engines during 1960, but this did not eradicate the problems. EE contended, though, that the class was achieving more than 90% availability outside the period spent having the engines changed. Over several years consideration was given more than once to fitting an EE SVT diesel, and this was expanded to installing a production series Deltic 18-cylinder unit that would have pushed the class into the Type 3 category.

EE quoted for refurbishment of the class on 4 September 1962 (Contract CCR 1351). By 1963 all were out of traffic and were eventually moved to Vulcan for the work to be carried out. This covered just about all aspects of the locomotive and included a further rebuild by Napier of the 'Deltic' engines. No D5904 was the first to emerge during April 1964 and went to Doncaster Works for trial running to Grantham and Peterborough. No D5901 was the last to be completed on 14 April 1965. One aspect of the work was repainting into Type 5 'Deltic' two-tone green livery.

Above left: **Young admirers observe No D5901 as it brings empty stock into King's Cross on 19 September 1959. Note one of the observers has a pencil behind his ear, a sight, like the 'Baby Deltic', that one does not see today!** *R. A. Panting*

Left: **On 12 October 1959 No D5907 stands at Hitchin with an up Cambridge Buffet Car express.** *A. E. Baker*

Above: **Nose-end train headcode panels replaced the gangway doors during refurbishment. No D5904 (left) and No D6903 sit at the King's Cross buffer stops on 15 August 1968 following arrival with the 07.48 from Hertford and 07.15 from Royston respectively.** *D. L. Percival*

The overhauled examples had hardly returned to traffic when a number of problems arose with the radiators, and these persisted for nearly three years, despite a range of options being tried. The culling of non-standard types under the National Traction Plan included Class 23, and engine overhauls were halted by BR in May 1968. Thus, although the refurbishment work had been generally successful and delivered availability figures of between 80 and 90%, withdrawals commenced in September 1968 and were completed by March 1971. No D5901 had a new career in store, however, because it was acquired by the Railway Technical Centre at Derby to haul test trains. Its final use came in late 1975 and official withdrawal followed in October 1976. All the class were scrapped.

EE Type 2 'Baby Deltics'

Length	52ft 6in
Width	8ft 10¾in
Height	12ft 8in
Weight	74 tons
Wheel diameter	3ft 7in
Engine	Napier 'Deltic' T9-29
Engine output	1,100bhp at 1,600rpm
Maximum speed	75mph
Tractive effort, maximum	47,000lb
continuous	30,600lb at 9.4mph
Gear ratio	63:17
Fuel tank capacity	450 gallons
Minimum curve radius 4 chains	

D5900-9 carried English Electric Co Rotation Numbers 2377-2386, together with Vulcan Foundry Works Numbers D417-26.

BR/Sulzer D5000 series (later Class 24)

BR's workshops were keen to participate in diesel locomotive building to the point where some wished to design and construct their own engines and electrical machines. Fortunately the latter idea never gained credence because research and development is very costly, well beyond railway resources. Derby Works had designed and built the two LMS prototypes, Nos 10000/1, using EE equipment, and there was logic in allocating orders to the Works under the Pilot Scheme. J. F. Harrison, the LMR CME, was known to favour Sulzer diesels, while that company had not forged an alliance with any other locomotive builder, and was naturally happy to collaborate with Derby. By the time tenders were called for, Sulzer's LDA28 'A' series diesel was developing 193hp per cylinder at 750rpm, and this meant the six-cylinder in-line version would produce 1,160bhp; in twin-bank 12-cylinder form it would develop 2,300bhp. The LMR was attracted to having just two diesel classes, which would use this one engine in either the six- or twelve-cylinder arrangement.

Derby approached BTH for the electrical machines, the main generator being 12-pole model RTB15656, continuously rated at 735kW, 1,400A, 525V at 750rpm. The 8-pole 32/50kW auxiliary generator was the RTB 7440. The traction motors were type 137BY, continuously rated at 213shp, 350A, 525V at 549rpm, and were mounted conventionally, connected in parallel across the main generator. Gearing was fairly low to reflect the envisaged duties and this gave a predicted continuous rating speed of 13.5mph, later revised to 14.8mph.

A strength underframe was used, with aluminium for parts of the superstructure to save weight, which was quoted at the time as 75 tons in working order, just on the specified limit. This was quickly found to be 79.8 tons, and subsequent builds incorporated additional weight-saving measures, reducing the weight to 73 tons. Unlike EE with its Class 23s, no pressure appears to have been put on Derby Works to bring its prototypes within the specified weight limit. Bodyside air filters detracted somewhat from the overall styling effect, and cab-front gangway doors were fitted. The class also had the Blue Star coupling code. Standard BR green was applied to most of the superstructure, with a grey roof. The official photograph of the class

Above: **The official British Railways photograph of BR Type 2 No D5010 illustrates the bodyside cluttered with grilles, which should be compared to the more stylish BRCW Type 2.** *British Railways*

Left: **Most of the Pilot Scheme batch were sent to the SR from new to allow steam to be withdrawn on the South East Division's Kent Coast services. They remained there until the SR's own diesel type, the BRCW Type 3 D6500 series, finally arrived. This summer-dated service, the 7.55am Birkenhead Woodside to Margate, had probably travelled up the ex-GWR main line as far as Reading, before being photographed leaving Redhill on 15 June 1959. It would be interesting to know where Nos D5001 and D5009 have taken over the train.** *Stanley Creer*

Above: The sight of a BR Type 2 at Folkestone Warren, without third-rail electrification, seems incongruous today. In May 1959 No D5010 is on the same working from Margate. *Derek Cross*

Above right: Back from the Southern, No D5015 departs from Manchester Central for Liverpool Central on 4 June 1960. Services between these cities had been the preserve of 4MT 2-6-4T steam locomotives for many years, so this was exactly the sort of work for which the new diesels were designed. *John K. Morton*

Right: The modestly powered Type 2 No D5012 has to fit in with the 'big boys' on the up fast along the West Coast line as it climbs Whitmore bank near Madeley with a Liverpool Lime Street to Birmingham New Street service on 16 June 1962. *R. J. Farrell*

doyen shows it with a narrow white band at mid-height that extended around the whole body. However, at some stage in the construction programme later builds had a broad band above the solebar, which also extended around the whole body. The class was numbered D5000-19.

In 1957 a further 10 were ordered for deployment on the ER. Although planned for LMR utilisation, even before construction had been completed it was arranged that 15 locomotives would be sent to the SR to eliminate Kent Coast steam diagrams ahead of electrification; this was before the delivery of an order for diesels specifically for that Region. No D5000 emerged from Derby Works in July 1958 and was exhibited at Marylebone on the 24th. On 15 August the locomotive took a 15-coach test train from Derby to Liverpool via Cheadle Junction.

Shortly afterwards No D5000 was put to work on a passenger diagram that started at Derby Midland with the 9.28am to Manchester Central. From there it took a train forward to Liverpool Central before working its way back to Derby. Entry to capital stock is reported as taking place on 5 September, allocated to Crewe South, to which all 20 went initially.

During November 1959 No D5008 was put through full road trials using both the LMR's mobile test units and the dynamometer car. By virtue of the main generator characteristic, the maximum starting tractive effort was established to be 40,000lb, as predicted, but the continuous rating figure was higher than predicted at 22,700lb. Full engine output was available between 9.3 and 58.3mph, the latter figure lower than predicted, and peak transmission efficiency was 79.2%.

Above: **The nine-coach 7am Lowestoft to Birmingham New Street forms a substantial load for a 1,160bhp locomotive on express timings, which speaks volumes for the schedules appertaining at the time. No D5005 passes Stechford Junction on the Birmingham outskirts on 8 September 1962.**
M. Mensing

Right: **With the demise of the NBL Type 2s, many of the BR Pilot Scheme Type 2s migrated north of the border to see out their days. On 29 August 1973 No 5003 finds itself with a parcels train on the former GSWR main line near Auchinleck.**
Tom Heavyside

The control system and engine governor combined to give a good level of fuel efficiency and the overall results were regarded as satisfactory.

Deliveries progressed steadily, with No D5019 entering service on 11 July 1959. Between January 1959 and June 1962 Nos D5000-14 were based at Hither Green for a range of duties on the SR's South Eastern Division. It was then that the locomotive was discovered to be five tons overweight, causing the SR Civil Engineer to impose a number of restrictions on routes and utilisation. Nos D5002-6 had their boilers removed to save weight. Inexplicably, on 7 October 1961, No D5000 appears to have been given the honour of being the first diesel to work a boat train from Southampton Docks to Waterloo, a duty well outside its normal sphere of operation.

Meanwhile Nos D5015-9 made appearances on the Midland line until

These pictures illustrate how varied and widespread were the passenger assignments allocated to the BR Type 2s. Here Nos D5018 and D5019, on outer-suburban services from the old Euston station, take centre stage, with an ex-LMS 'Black Five' in the background.
Ian Allan Library

Renumbered to No 24009, the former D5009 trundles through Stirling on 25 May 1974 with a short freight. *Tom Heavyside*

taking over suburban services out of Euston from the Winter 1959 timetable, these duties lasting until Summer 1961.

On returning to the LMR, they were split between London area sheds and Crewe South. Some, including No D5000, saw out their days on the LMR, becoming redundant from 1969 onwards, although No D5000, renumbered to No 24005, was not actually withdrawn until 31 January 1976. Others (sometimes after being in store for two years) found a new lease of life for a short while in Scotland, where Polmadie took them as replacements for NBL Type 2s during 1971, with a subsequent transfer to Eastfield. No D5001 was the exception and remained an LMR machine until withdrawal in October 1975, the end date for most of the survivors; it had been at Crewe depot since 1966. No D5009 (by then No 24009) was the last on BR's books and went in July 1976. None now survive.

In service the Sulzer engine gave little trouble, after a manufacturing change to the pistons, incorporated by Vickers, which was reversed to the standard Sulzer pattern. Siting the engine room air intakes along the bodyside, especially low down, caused more dirt to be drawn inside and this resulted in greater engine wear than on the equivalent design by BRCW, which will be discussed next. In later builds of the BR/Sulzer Type 2 these air intake grilles were moved to cantrail level. The electrical equipment was generally trouble-free, but there were perhaps a few issues of design detail, among them cab heating, that slightly marred the overall result. A total of 151 locomotives of this type were eventually built, while the 'B' version of the Sulzer engine was fitted to 327 examples that used the same main generator but different traction motors, being designated Class 25.

BR/Sulzer Type 2

Length	50ft 6in
Width	9ft 1in
Height	12ft 8in
Weight	79 tons 16cwt
Wheel diameter	3ft 9in
Engine	Sulzer 6LDA28A
Engine output	1,160bhp at 750rpm
Maximum speed	75mph
Tractive effort,	
maximum	40,000lb
continuous	21,300lb at 14.8 mph
Gear ratio	81:16
Fuel tank capacity	630 gallons
Minimum curve radius	4½ chains

D5000-19 were built under BR Derby Order D251.

BRCW D5300 series (later Class 26)

BRCW also teamed up with Sulzer to produce this design of Type B locomotive, with Crompton Parkinson providing the electrical machines. Thus the same 6LDA28A power plant as that fitted to Class 24 was married to a CG391A1 10-pole main generator, continuously rated at 757kW, 1,720A, 440V at 750rpm, with an overhung 8-pole CAG193A1 auxiliary generator, continuously rated at 57kW, 518A, 110V at 450/750rpm. Four 4-pole C171A1 traction motors continuously rated at 224hp, 430A, 440V at 340rpm were fitted, and were connected in parallel across the main generator. Having as many as five stages of field weakening no doubt helped to ensure that full engine output was available between 7 and 75mph. The BR Diagram Book shows a maximum speed of 75mph, but the locomotives were stencilled in service for 80mph.

Traditional construction methods were employed but with greater attention to detailed styling than with Class 24. Hence the engine room air intakes were at cantrail level and the front end was less plain, helped by the use of off-white paint for the cab window surrounds. Traditional BR green was used for the body, coupled with a grey roof and grey waistband line. The class became Nos D5300-19 and had the more common Blue Star coupling code. The contract price was £63,037, but ended up costing £71,704.

The clean lines of BRCW's Type 2 are evident here as class doyen No D5300 approaches Palmers Green with a local from King's Cross on 1 September 1958. *British Railways*

Once based on the Scottish Region, the BRCW Type 2s strayed on to LMR metals quite regularly. One route used for these forays was the Waverley from Edinburgh to Carlisle. On 25 May 1962 No D5316 passes Falahill Junction.
Derek Cross

Destined for the ER, Doncaster undertook the acceptance trials as each locomotive was handed over by the builder. No D5300 left Smethwick Works during early August 1958 and was noted heading south along the East Coast line on the 6th. Curiously, one source gives a date to traffic of 30 July 1958, with allocation to Hornsey. It was joined there in September by No D5301, and both were used on King's Cross to Hitchin outer-suburban Class 2 trains. No D5319 followed its predecessors to Hornsey, to complete the order in March 1959, and all the class migrated to Finsbury Park during April 1960 when that depot opened.

No D5303 was noted on 3 October 1958 on the 11.30am Birmingham New Street to Newcastle train, ex-works and bound for Doncaster for acceptance. On 29 October the same machine was noted passing Newcastle with a train bound for Leith. It then spent several weeks on trials north of the Border, returning to Carlisle on 15 November on the 12 noon from Edinburgh Waverley. The same month saw the class appearing at Moorgate via the Widened Lines on passenger trains, but they were banned from going further south via Snow Hill Tunnel on freight because the SR deemed them (like Class 24) to be overweight. Meanwhile BRCW was building against repeat orders for a

further 27 examples, but it also had to contend with returns from the Pilot Scheme batch for modification.

The stay on the Great Northern proved short, with displacement once the Brush Type 2s had been delivered in sufficient numbers. During April and May 1960 there was a steady migration into Scotland for use north of Edinburgh, when 18 locomotives were rostered for 16 diagrams. When the Scottish Region wanted to convert the shipment of coal between the Fife area and Cockenzie power station to MGR operation, there was no prospect of receiving suitable Type 4 traction. Instead it converted Nos D5300-7 to have train air brake and slow speed control equipment to work the trains. The train-heating boiler and associated water tank were removed, reducing the overall weight to 75 tons; the maximum speed was 75mph, as opposed to 80mph for the rest of the class.

BR ordered a further design from BRCW with the 'B' series Sulzer engine and GEC equipment. Despite being less powerful and slower, Class 26 outlived its newer cousins into the 1990s, largely because its Crompton Parkinson machines were more reliable. In fact, the class was always regarded as a better performer than Class 24, despite having the same engine. No D5300 was renumbered as No 26007, while

The old North British Railway extended its tentacles south of the Solway and into Cumbria as far as Silloth on the coast. The low-rise building at Kirkandrews, the first station out of Carlisle, was typical of the company's style. On 30 August 1964 No D5305 rolls in with a down train. *Derek Cross*

No D5307 became No 26020, otherwise the last digit of the original number was retained by locomotives on renumbering.

Haymarket depot took care of maintenance until the 1990s when Eastfield took over. Nos 26001/2/4/7/10/11/14 all survive in preservation, another testimony to the usefulness and quality of the design. Aside from the early piston problems and a few teething troubles, this proved to be the second best of the Pilot Scheme order after the EE Type A.

BRCW Type 2

Length	50ft 9in
Width	8ft 10in
Height	12ft 8in
Weight	77 ton 17cwt
Wheel diameter	3ft 7in
Engine	Sulzer 6LDA28A
Engine output	1,160bhp at 750rpm
Maximum speed	75mph
Tractive effort,	
maximum	42,000lb
continuous	30,000lb at 11$\frac{1}{4}$mph
Gear ratio	63:16
Fuel tank capacity	500 gallons
Minimum curve radius	5 chains

D5300-19 carried BRCW Co Works Nos DEL 45-64.

Metropolitan Vickers D5700 series (later Class 28)

For two reasons, this was the most unusual of the Pilot Scheme designs. While enthusiasts focus on the choice of a Co-Bo wheel arrangement as marking out the type, in fact the really distinctive feature was the use of a conventional two-stroke diesel, the only such application of this arrangement to run on BR until the General Motors (GM) Class 59s arrived in the 1980s. Until very recently GM developed (and largely perfected) a range of two-stroke prime movers that contrasted with those of most other manufacturers, who preferred a diesel that used a four-stroke cycle. Although a shortage of foreign currency, and lobbying from British manufacturers, precluded the BTC from buying GM engines for use in the Pilot Scheme, the success of that company's products made the trial of a locally manufactured two-stroke a worthwhile proposition.

Oliver Bulleid, who had been the CME of the Southern Railway until nationalisation, had subsequently been appointed to the equivalent post at Irish Railways (CIE). Rather than modernise the latter's motive power with new steam locomotives, he moved in the diesel direction. Having heard very good reports from the Admiralty about

Left: **Although Peterhead lost its passenger service during May 1965, goods traffic survived until 7 September 1970. On 9 September what is described as the final train sits in the station behind No D5307.** *Derek Cross*

Below left: **Staying in Great North of Scotland Railway territory, this time at Dyce Junction, on 22 November 1973, No 5309 struggles a little with the 11.35 fish train from Fraserburgh to Aberdeen, the only daily train along the Buchan branch.** *Brian Morrison*

Below: **Bleak scenery at Dalnaspidal on the Highland line surrounds Nos 26012 and 26019 as they head for Inverness with a train of coal on 17 June 1980.** *Tom Heavyside*

Far left: While on its first trial run, hauling 14 coaches from Stockton-on-Tees to Leeds on 7 July 1958, Metrovick Type 2 No D5700, in primer paint, joins the Church Fenton to Harrogate route at Wetherby West Junction from the Leeds direction. *Metrovick*

Left: When British Railways decided to try a new freight venture that involved carrying small containers between North London and Glasgow, the Metrovick Type 2s were assigned to the duty. On 1 October 1958 Nos D5700 and D5701 made a trial run, seen here on the Midland line. *Metrovick, taken from a company publicity book*

the reliability of the Crossley two-stroke diesel, coupled with a design for Western Australia that used this engine within a locomotive built by Metrovick, Bulleid felt confident in ordering 60 machines for CIE on 5 May 1954. Crossley's HSTV8 engine, rated at 1,200bhp continuously, and 1,320bhp for 1 hour, at 625rpm, was matched to Metrovick electrical machines. Construction of these Irish locomotives was by Metropolitan-Cammell at part of the former Great Central Carriage & Wagon Works at Dukinfield, Manchester, which was rented from British Railways for the purpose. These 60 examples had a Co-Co wheel arrangement for a weight of 82 tons, and were geared for 75mph, deliveries commencing in mid-1955.

The Crossley engine was a simple design, unlike the GM products, which were more sophisticated, or, perhaps, more highly developed. Crossley had not devoted as much resource into similar development, in part because this had not been required, based on service experience, and in part to keep development costs low, rather than look for technical improvement. Admiralty use would have been at a generally constant loading, whereas rail applications involve constant cycling of power to meet varying requirements during a journey. The Navy would also usually have engineering personnel close at hand to attend to any issues that might arise during operation, which was not the case with rail. Metrovick had an impeccable reputation for quality electrical machines and had constructed locomotives for export. All these factors combined to support an order from that company under the Pilot Scheme. Railway staff always referred to the type as the 'Crossleys', whereas enthusiasts dubbed them the 'Co-Bos', after the wheel arrangement.

Metrovick had formed an alliance with Beyer Peacock for locomotive production and this had brought the setting-up of a factory at Stockton-on-Tees, which was where the Type Bs for BR were built. Having carried out construction of a design for CIE that employed the same engine and electrical equipment, it is (at this time) surprising to see such a divergence from the mechanical parts between the two types. If the BTC wanted a Type B with an $18\frac{3}{4}$-ton axle load, then the CIE design would have fitted the bill admirably. Instead, what emerged was a locomotive with a $19\frac{3}{4}$-ton maximum axle

After refurbishment, the 'Crossleys' (as BR staff termed the class) went to Cumbria. On 15 August 1964 No D5715 powers away from Carnforth in charge of a Workington to Manchester Victoria train.
Derek Cross

load. Metrovick's publicity leaflet gives the maximum and continuous rating tractive effort values as 50,000lb and 25,000lb respectively, and goes on to say that 'it is these basic requirements that have led to the adoption of the five-axle, five-motor design'.

Access to the cab was via a door on the secondman's side, or a driver's-side door set behind the cab. Locating the latter door away from the cab was intended to reduce it as a source of cab draughts. Wrap-around windows were fitted in the cabs to offer better visibility. The driver's power controller, which had 10 fixed notches, followed Continental practice in being a wheel, rather than a handle.

Construction followed the traditional strength underframe approach. BR staff who knew the class all report that they were built like tanks and, perhaps understandably, gave a hard but comfortable ride. Cab-front gangway doors for inter-locomotive access, when working in multiple, were provided. The Crossley engine had a Metrovick TG4204 8-pole main generator attached, which was continuously rated at 802/783kW, 1,070/1,650A, 750/475V at 625rpm. Interestingly, the BR Drivers Handbook *BR 33003/55*, a revision of November 1965, gives the TG4204's continuous rating as 802/790kW, 1,070/1,520A, 750/520V at 625rpm, as a rating revision must have been issued. A Metrovick AG103AZ auxiliary generator was fitted, rated at 62kW, 565A, 110V between 400 and 625rpm. By virtue of the Co-Bo wheel arrangement, there were five Metrovick 137BZ 4-pole traction motors, rated at 180hp, 330A, 475V at 510rpm. Employing two stages of field weakening in the motors enabled full engine output to be available between 4.3 and 61mph.

No livery description has emerged during research, but the basic body colour was BR green. A broad eggshell-blue band extended between the entrance doors, and this colour might also have been used for the bodyside grilles. The wheel tyres had white rims and this was also applied to part of the bogies. Some of the undergear was also painted eggshell blue. It seems that the BTC permitted each manufacturer to adopt such minor flourishes within the overall corporate green style. The 20 examples were numbered D5700-19 and the final price per locomotive was £78,488.

Deliveries began on 2 July 1958, with Nos D5700/1 going to Thornaby shed for weighing before a programme of trial running. On the 7th the class doyen was taken on a circuit from Stockton to Leeds, hauling 14 coaches, and this showed up some teething difficulties. Eight days later

it hauled a 13-car load around Tyneside, but, confusingly, another report gives this as the date it arrived at Derby; with No D5701, for driver training along the Churnet Valley route through Leek. No D5700 was finally accepted by BR on the 26th, No D5719 concluding the build on 17 October 1959.

By 1 October 1958 Nos D5700/1 were regulars in multiple on Derby to St Pancras expresses. As a prelude to a new freight service, on that date Nos D5700/1 made a trial run on a 25-wagon consist that conveyed mini-containers, two per vehicle. The service, named the 'Condor' ('Containers Door-to-Door'), was launched on 16 March 1959 between Hendon, North London (departing 7.23pm), and Gushetfaulds, Glasgow, on a 10-hour schedule. Pairs of 'Crossleys' provided the motive power and it is believed the cab-front interconnecting

When they moved north, the 'Co-Bos', as enthusiasts always refer to them, went first to Carlisle Kingmoor for a short time, then Barrow and finally back to Kingmoor to see out their final months. No D5707 is pictured here on a freight at Kingmoor Yard.
Derek Cross

doors were used to allow footplate staff to move between locomotives.

Polmadie shed was used for stabling and this led to a range of work being performed before returning south in the evening: among others, there were trips on Glasgow Central to Greenock and Glasgow St Enoch to Carlisle passenger turns. Alternatively, the class was deployed on the 9.15am Bridgeton Yard to Stirling train, less than 4 hours after arriving at Gushetfaulds, following the 400-mile trip from London — intensive operating indeed! The 'Condor' loadings failed to justify a pair, and by October 1959 a single 'Crossley' was being diagrammed.

The class became regular performers in pairs on expresses from St Pancras to Derby and Manchester Central or singly on local services. In January 1960 No D5707 worked a 7.57am Harpenden to Moorgate service, with other subsequent sightings on commuter trains to and from Moorgate. More new ground was broken by No

Like the other two-stroke diesels used on BR (the 'Deltics'), the Crossley-engined Metrovicks were prone to smoke, especially after being left with the engine idling for any length of time. On 13 April 1966 No D5707 takes the road towards Barrow at Dalton Junction with the 11.25am Euston to Windermere train. *D. A. Idle*

Typical Victorian architecture of the area flanks No D5708 and its Workington Main to Carnforth stopper on one side, with the Irish Sea on the other. The location is between Sellafield and Seascale and the date is 31 July 1963.
R. J. Farrell

D5714 on 4 April when it appeared at Norwood Yard and was borrowed for trips to Three Bridges on both the 6th and 7th.

In the February 1959 *Trains Illustrated* Cecil J. Allen provided an interesting comparison between Class 6 and 7 steam power and a pair of 'Crossleys' between St Pancras and Kettering. The two Class 6 'Jubilees' were limited to 300 tons on 'XL' timings, and both the featured runs marginally exceeded this. The Class 7 'Royal Scot' took 450 tons gross and the 'Crossleys' were in charge of 390 tons — nine, 12 and 11 coaches respectively. The diesels were much quicker getting away from the London terminus, not least because steam drivers sensibly allowed time for the fire to burn through before maximum efforts were demanded. Up the 1 in 170 to West Hampstead the four trains attained 44, 38, 40 and 55mph respectively. The latter suggests 1,700rhp by the Crossleys, against 1,800 predicted.

Two of the steam performances were then hampered by a track slowing, but the third went through Hendon at 61 in order to rush the succeeding climb to Elstree. By contrast the diesels passed Hendon at only 63mph. Five miles at 1 in 176 to Elstree gave the honours to the Class 6 'Jubilee' runs, with minima of 55 and 59, whereas the 'Crossleys' fell to 58½mph, again suggesting 1,700rhp. On the long, sweeping downgrades that are a feature of this route, all the steam drivers approached or exceeded 90mph, whereas the diesels were held within their 75mph ceiling, showing the short-sightedness of the BTC in specifying such a low limit. Later Type 2s were designed for 90mph. By virtue of the faster running, one of the 'Jubilee' drivers achieved the best net start-to-stop time of 66½ minutes to Kettering (72 miles). The other 'Jubilee' driver tied with the 'Crossleys' at 67¼ minutes and the 'Royal Scot' managed just under 71 minutes, all well within the booked schedule.

Problems with the Crossley engines became apparent very quickly and probably mirrored those suffered by their Irish equivalents. It is possible that the latter, having been in service three years before the BR 'Crossleys', had already

The D5700s split their time between passenger and freight work. Towards the end of its life, No D5712 threads the Lune Gorge at Dillicar with a ballast train for Carlisle. *David Wharton*

shown up trouble and this may have been a factor in BR deciding in November 1958 not to replicate the design. Stress cracking was affecting one corner of the engine crankcase and, it is said, by June 1960 only three examples were serviceable. By October pairs were again back on Midland-line expresses, as well as the 'Condor'. Due to continuing problems during 1961, the class was put into store at several locations, notably Derby, pending a decision on what to do next. Average mileages reflect time out of traffic, being only 37,184 in 1959, 24,385 in 1960 and 3,647 in 1961.

Eventually agreement was reached for a programme of major work that was carried out at the former Great Central Carriage & Wagon Works at Dukinfield, ironically where their Irish antecedents had been built. As with the Class 303

Glasgow 'Blue Trains' before them, this facility provided an out-of-the-way location for the work, with AEI (the merged Metrovick and BTH), Crossley and BR staff collaborating on the project. Although described as refurbishment, most of the work centred on the engine, with the fitting of a new crankcase that was strengthened at the corner where it had been prone to fracture. New pistons, injectors and hoses were fitted, and new iron cylinder heads replaced the original aluminium ones. Although this increased the locomotive weight, no one said anything about this!

The Spanner train-heating boiler had been prone to cut out due to ventilation problems in one direction of travel, so a duplicate set of control relays was fitted to cure the problem. The compressor unloading valve was prone to stick and this was solved by the use of a governor valve used on the Drewry shunters. The wrap-around cab windows had been difficult to procure, so a revised flat windscreen was fitted. The three parties to the work had to agree which organisation would bear the cost for each locomotive, and this was done on site by the local representatives by way of weekly sheets. BR found, however, that AEI was cheating by adding work to be booked to BR once the sheets had been signed!

No D5702 seems to have gone through the programme first, leaving Derby on 18 October, being joined over the next two days by Nos D5700/1/5/6/11/14-18. As each locomotive came off works it was sent to Gorton shed for a loaded trial trip. This was made over the Midland line to the Leicester area with 10 coaches. Concurrently, the nearby Beyer Peacock works was turning out Type 3 'Hymek' diesel-hydraulics, but these took only eight bogies during their trial run, to ensure that the locomotive achieved sufficient speed for the hydraulic transmission to operate in all its ranges. The foreman at Ashburys carriage sidings would be told to arrange a rake of stock for a locomotive trial, but used to get confused as to what size of train he had to provide!

The railway had moved on by the time the 'Crosslevs' had been refurbished, and their former duties had been taken over by new BR/Sulzer Type 4s. Instead of returning to Derby, the class was sent instead to work around Cumbria, based at Carlisle Upperby from February 1962, then at Barrow-in-Furness from September 1963. Just before their demise, however, came a further move back to Carlisle's Kingmoor diesel depot. Concentration in Cumbria kept crew training to a minimum and also less in the public eye. Here deployment was on freight and secondary passenger, with visits to Manchester on the service from Workington.

Unfortunately the engine again caused trouble, with cracking of the crankcase at the opposite corner to the previous problem area. The shedmaster at Barrow

was quizzed as to the duties being assigned to the class and responded that these were 'light'. Checking revealed an operating regime of up to 22 hours per day, and when challenged that this was not 'light', the shedmaster retorted that the trains were not heavy!

By way of a 'fix', a $1\frac{1}{4}$-inch stud was inserted to put that corner of the crankcase under pressure. One example, No D5705, was fitted with a fresh crankcase from Crossley. Consideration was also given to re-engining the whole fleet, and EE's 8CSVT unit was proposed, set to deliver 1,350bhp; this was a charge-cooled version of the unit fitted in the EE Type 1. Metrovick was confident that the electrical machines would be able to cope with up to 1,800bhp. In fact, save for one major main generator flashover, the electrical machines had given exemplary service. Although flashovers did occur, these were so minor as to merely require the driver to reset the overload trip. Like the 'Deltic' two-stroke engines, during periods of idling, unburnt oil had a tendency to collect in the silencer. Once put on full power for a sustained period, the silencer would get hot and the unburnt oil would ignite, giving a pyrotechnic display through the roof.

Curiously, the 'Crosslevs' were selected for use on the ICI limestone trains between Tunstead in the Peak District and Northwich. They were to be used singly and based at Trafford Park shed, with return visits to Barrow for maintenance. Although driver training took place, this sphere of operation proved short-lived, and the class was displaced by Sulzer Type 2s. As with so many of the Pilot Scheme designs, the 1967 National Traction Plan regarded the 'Crosslevs' as non-standard and surplus.

No D5709 had been out of traffic at Crewe Works since January 1965, some six years after being delivered new. Nos D5704/10/13/15 were also taken to Crewe during 1966, pending the start of the re-engining scheme that never materialised. Nevertheless, during 1967 Crewe Works continued to carry out repairs on other class members, while No D5701 even underwent a classified overhaul and received Rail Blue livery during October and November.

Withdrawals came between December 1967 and 7 September 1968, with No D5705 reinstated in February 1969 for use by the Railway Technical Centre. By 1974 this requirement ended and the locomotive was converted for use as a carriage heating unit, initially at Gloucester, then Swansea and finally at Bristol, from where it was withdrawn on 11 January 1980 and taken to Swindon Works for asbestos removal and acquisition for preservation. Initial restoration work took place on Peak Rail, but the locomotive later moved to the East Lancs Railway at Bury. Bringing the story full circle, it is possible that components from Metrovick's original contract for Western Australia may find their way into No D5705; it seems that the engine problems in the export machines were overcome and the type survived into the 1990s, so compatible engine components may see future use back in the UK. An HSTV8 engine has now been sourced from a generating or pumping station in Canada and should enable restoration to be completed.

Metrovick Type 2	
Length	56ft 7½in
Width	9ft 2in
Height	12ft 8in
Weight	97 tons 3cwt
Wheel diameter	3ft 3½in
Engine	Crossley HSTV8
Engine output	1,200bhp at 625rpm
Maximum speed	75mph
Tractive effort,	
maximum	50,000lb
continuous	25,000lb at 13½mph
Gear ratio	67:15
Fuel tank capacity	510 gallons
Minimum curve radius	3½ chains

D5700-19 were allocated Metrovick Works Numbers 993-1012, though these were not present on the builder's plates.

Brush D5500 series (later Class 30)

In securing an order under the Pilot Scheme for 20 locomotives, Brush would have been assisted by virtue of having several very senior railway figures within its employ, including H. G. Ivatt. Its parent company had made funds available for a new locomotive erecting shop at Loughborough, together with test facilities. In 1950 Brush had secured an order for 25 locomotives for Ceylon Government Railway, and this basic design was a clear candidate for the Pilot Scheme, so 20 technically similar units were ordered.

Construction was under Brush Traction Contract No 04/45100 at £70,650 per locomotive, but the final cost was £78,043. Another part of the group of which Brush was part, W. G. Bagnall Ltd of Stafford, was contracted to build the underframes for Nos D5515-9. The same wheel arrangement as for the Ceylon order, A1A-A1A, was adopted, possibly to offer a low axle load and high route availability. This was, perhaps, fortunate because the overall weight turned out at 104 tons, as against 87 tons for the export order and less than 80 tons for most of the other Type 2s. Some modification of the Ceylon design was made to reflect differences in track and loading gauges and running requirements. Hence a 'Commonwealth'-pattern bogie was adopted.

A strength underframe was used, with cross-members being used to support the steel plate bodysides. A Mirrlees JVS12T engine was installed, rated at 1,250bhp at 850rpm. A Brush TG160-48 8-pole traction generator was mounted on the engine, continuously rated at 823kW, 686V, 1,200A at 850rpm. A Brush TG69-24 Mk I 6-pole auxiliary generator, rated at 30kW, 110V, 273A at 450/850rpm, was used. The A1A-A1A wheel arrangement means that there were four traction motors, mounted on each of the outermost bogie axles. These motors were of Brush TM73-68 4-pole type, rated at 250hp each at 600A, 343V, 485rpm, and were connected in two series-parallel

An interesting view of No D5503 at Liverpool Street. Judging by the relatively clean roof, the locomotive is either fairly new or not long off a repaint.
Ian Allan Library

pairs and had four stages of field weakening. Gearing was 64:17 and maximum speed was 75mph, later raised to 80. An electro-magnetic system of engine control meant that, for operating in multiple, the locomotives were given the Red Circle code.

The cab-front design differed from the nose ends used on the Ceylon build. The BTC Design Panel took a hand and produced a flat front, with two large and one small cab windows, the latter mounted over the usual gangway doors.

Livery was BR green for the body, grey for the roof, black for the undergear, with light grey waist and skirt bands extended around the locomotive, one at cab windscreen height that encompassed all the window surrounds, and the other above the solebar. Numbering was from D5500 to D5519.

No D5500 was completed in the last week of September 1957, with a trial run to Chinley on 10 October. It was allocated to Stratford on 31 October, which was home depot for most of the class for most

On introduction to traffic, the Brush Type 2s played understudy to the more powerful EE Type 4s on passenger jobs originating at Liverpool Street. No D5505 passes Brentwood with the 4.56pm down to Colchester on 24 May 1958.
Stanley Creer

The machine that was trialled at 1,400bhp for a time, No D5507, hurries down Brentwood bank on 14 June 1958 with an up express.
Stanley Creer

of their BR service. In fact, BR confined the depot allocation within the Great Eastern Section, since the first 20 Pilot Scheme build were non-standard with later orders because of their Red Circle multiple coupling code, as opposed to Blue Star.

As the BTC abandoned the Pilot Scheme concept by multiplying several designs before any had even been built, Brush was not one of the lucky ones. BR had decided to adopt its own Derby/Sulzer Type 2 (D5000 series) as the future standard, and in 1958 this, it is said, caused Brush to decide to pull out of locomotive construction. Early experience with the design, however, caused the ER to lobby for its replication. Shortage of capacity within BR's own workshops was a further factor in the decision to order 40 further examples, which prompted a policy change by Brush in favour of a resumption of locomotive building. How different the shape of BR over the ensuing three decades might have been if Falcon Works had not carried out any further construction!

During 1959 No D5516 was put through a full series of road trials along the Norwich main line. The locomotive had run 16,700 miles from new. Engine output was found to be virtually exactly the 1,250bhp rating, and the continuous rating of the main generator was 22,600lb at $16\frac{1}{2}$mph. Rail horsepower averaged 1,105 between 20 and 50mph, demonstrating quite a good transmission efficiency of 81%, while even at 80mph the transmission efficiency was still $76\frac{1}{2}$% at 960rhp. At 50mph the drawbar hp was 900, meaning that locomotive resistance was absorbing 205hp, and by 80mph the power required to move the locomotive was 540hp. At the latter speed, only 420hp was therefore available to haul the train, and one is left wondering why this figure should end up so low; certainly the need for 540hp to move the locomotive at 80mph seems inordinately high, and the author queries the way these locomotive resistance figures have been derived.

Maximum tractive effort was established as 51,000lb at 2,250A main

These two photographs show that the class was not confined to Liverpool Street passenger duties. As the advent of route electrification approaches, No D5517 (*above*) finds employment on the 12.10pm Shoeburyness to Fenchurch Street train on 7 August 1960. *M. Edwards*

Left: Meanwhile, 'out in the sticks' on 22 April 1960 the 1pm Ipswich to Cambridge service had No D5501 as motive power when captured on film near Newmarket. *H. Webb-Cornwall*

generator current, an adhesion factor of 31.6%, whereas the normal peak main generator current was 2,000A, at which tractive effort was 46,000lb; Brush predicted a value of 42,000lb. Without exceeding the continuous rating of the main generator, the tractive effort could be sustained at close to a safe drawbar limit during acceleration up to 7½mph.

Overall, the tests showed that the class operated close to its theoretical specification but was probably a little underpowered for the semi-fast passenger duties envisaged. The ability to cope with freights of up to 1,100 tons was established, though with such a heavy trailing load care was needed on the steepest inclines to avoid prolonged excess of the main generator continuous rating. During 1959 the class averaged

59,990 miles, dropping to 40,828 in 1960 and 40,251 in 1961.

Not long after construction, No D5507 was uprated to 1,400bhp and permitted a maximum of 85mph. Judged a success (and with No D5507 returned to its original rating), the first repeat order saw the engine uprated to 1,365bhp at 900rpm. Among subsequent re-orders, D5545 and Nos D5655-70 were rated at 1,600bhp at 950rpm, while D5835 temporarily received a charge-cooled Mirrlees engine that delivered 2,000bhp at 1,000rpm. During the first five years very few problems were experienced, and the main issues affecting the class appear to have been faults in the control gear and engine room and control cubicle ventilation. Eventually, though, piston seizures were experienced and were traced to a slight design change to the cylinder liners; crankcase failures then came soon afterwards around May 1962.

The cylinder liner issue was fairly easy to eradicate by eliminating a relieving groove near the top of the liner. Fracturing in the crankcase was, however, much more serious, and had two causes: the cylinder firing load caused fracturing at the foot of the cylinder housing (pointing to under-design of the structure in this area), and there was cracking of the bearing housings due to engine rotational speed. Fewer problems were experienced with the Pilot Scheme batch, suggesting that the uprating of the JVS12T diesel in later orders had caused excessive stresses. Similar problems had beset the same engines in Rhodesia, which had been rebuilt to a Mark 3 design and subsequently performed satisfactorily.

BR knew all about engine stress failures due to its experience with the Crossley-engined No D5700s, where a manufacturer's 'fix' had not resolved the problem. This may have coloured the railway's view of what to do, not least because this time the fleet size was 263, not 20. Faced with a serious potential drop in availability as major work was carried out on failed engines, BR came up with a fall-back plan. After considering the technical issues, it ordered 50 12SVT Mk 2 engines, set at 1,470bhp, from EE, which was Brush's chief competitor by this time.

This was an interesting decision and the reasoning has never fully been made public. One version says that this rating represented the limit of the cooler group, another that this was to avoid changes to the electrical machines. Of course, several examples of the class had been running at 1,600bhp and 2,000bhp for several years. Equally, the choice of a 12-cylinder SVT, rather than an eight-cylinder CSVT, is interesting. The latter, with its 1,350bhp output, would have more closely matched the performance of the production series D5500s and avoided an increase in overall weight. The 12SVT was less demanding on the engine when set at 1,470bhp, but had 50% more cylinders to maintain and pushed up locomotive weight by 3 tons.

Locomotives were given the EE power unit during classified overhauls, starting with No D5677 in March 1965. BR then decided not to send the Mirrlees engines rendered spare back for conversion to the Mark 3 pattern, but to opt for a campaign re-engining programme for all the fleet, selling off the redundant JSV12Ts. The Pilot Scheme examples were the last to be dealt with because they suffered less, having retained the original 1,250bhp setting. Under the TOPS classification, machines with Mirrlees units became Class 30, those from the Pilot Scheme batch with EE engines became Class 31/0, and the production batch with EE engines Class 31/1. Re-engining offered an opportunity to address a few design faults, including fitting an EE-pattern fuel delivery system. In December 1965 Class 31/1 was said to be achieving 94.7% availability.

No D5500 was renumbered under TOPS as No 31018 because No D5518 had been rebuilt in 1968 as a Class 31/1, as a result of sustaining collision damage to both cabs the previous year. No D5519 completed the class when it joined its sisters at Stratford in December 1958.

Looking at a journey published by Cecil

When the slightly uprated 1,365bhp variants of the Brush Type 2 arrived in large numbers, the lower-powered Pilot Scheme batch were downgraded more to freight duties. On 14 May 1968 No D5505 finds itself in unfamiliar third-rail territory at Brixton on a cross-London train of tanks.
J. H. Cooper-Smith

J. Allen in *Trains Illustrated* in March 1959, No D5513, with a nine-car, 330-ton load did not quite live up to the standard of the trial running. It must be assumed that between Norwich and Ipswich the locomotive was driven pretty much flat out all the way, judging by the demands of the schedule and speeds made by other motive power of higher capability. Nevertheless, in getting under way from Norwich No D5513 was producing only around 800rhp past Swainsthorpe. Nothing higher than 69mph was reached to Ipswich, where arrival in 48min 51sec was just over 2 minutes early.

Continuing to Liverpool Street, time was just about being maintained, top speed being 68mph through Chadwell Heath. The climb after Shenfield was spoiled by signals, but to that point 900rhp was developed at 59mph, again a little low. Further delays plagued the rest of the run. Between Norwich and Ipswich the Type 2s were allowed 51 minutes, as opposed to 45 for an EE Type 4. Continuing to London, the schedules were 77 and 73 minutes respectively.

Class 31/0 spent most of its BR days operating off Stratford depot, initially on passenger duties alongside EE Type 4 D200s and Type 3 D6700s from Liverpool Street to Norwich, Cambridge and King's Lynn. They became known as 'Toffee Apples' because their power controller was a spherical knob affixed to a vertical shaft. Gradually they became less preferred on passenger turns and were kept busy instead on local freight and engineer's traffic emanating from Temple Mills and other East London yards and terminals. By virtue of becoming surplus to requirements, withdrawals began in October 1976 with Nos 31001/9-11/16/18 all withdrawn on 10 July 1976; Nos 31012/14 followed later that year. A few were kept to serve in Departmental use as train-heating units, while No D5500 was accepted by the National Railway Museum as part of the National Collection. Nos 31002-6/8/15/17/19 all lasted into 1980, the end finally coming for the last three during October.

Changeling No D5518 became No 31101 and also hung around East Anglian depots until a move to Immingham in 1976, Thornaby in 1979 and back to Immingham in January 1981. Although withdrawn soon afterwards, on 3 May, remarkably it was selected for overhaul as a replacement for No 31314 and returned to traffic at Thornaby on 21 November 1982. In March 1984 it moved to Toton and around several other LMR depots until BR Sectorisation of motive power brought it back to Immingham in January 1988 as a Departmental machine. Just over a year later, the celebrity became Railfreight Speedlink property at Crewe Diesel, then, remarkably, Provincial Sector for passenger use. In November 1989 a final transfer came to Departmental as part of the Derby RTC pool, at Bescot. The final passenger action was on 10 August 1991 on Manchester to North Wales services, although withdrawal only came on 11 January 1993. It survives in preservation.

Although the Pilot Scheme examples were quite long-lived, the production Class 31/1s have proved extremely enduring and several continue to see main-line service. This is probably due to having the EE SVT engine installed, offering a useful 1,470bhp, with commonality of components across several classes. Reliable electrical equipment was also, no doubt, a factor, as was a class size of 263. Such longevity cannot be judged a failure, yet the need to replace the original Mirrlees engine put the design on a par with the oft-criticised 'Crossleys'.

By virtue of their Red Circle coupling code, the 'Toffee Apples' could work only in multiple together and not with later D5500s. Nos D5519 and D5513 find employment on a permanent way train at Leigh-on-Sea, Essex, on 12 February 1967. *D Mackinnon*

Brush Type 2

Length	56ft 9in
Width	8ft 9in
Height	12ft 7½in
Weight, as built	104 tons 7cwt
re-engined	107 tons
Wheel diameter, powered	3ft 7in
Non-powered	3ft 3½in
Engine, as built	Mirrlees JVS12T
re-engined	EE 12SVT Mark 2
Engine output, as built	1,250bhp at 850rpm
re-engined	1,470bhp at 850rpm
Maximum speed, original	75mph
revised	80mph
Tractive effort, as built,	
maximum	42,000lb
continuous	22,400lb at 16.5mph
as rebuilt, maximum	42,800lb
continuous	22,250lb at 19.7mph
Gear ratio	64:17
Fuel tank capacity	550 gallons
Minimum curve radius	4½ chains

D5500-04 carried Brush Traction Works Numbers 71-75 of 1957.
D5505-19 carried Brush Traction Works Numbers 76-90 of 1958.
W. G. Bagnall Ltd Works Numbers for the underframes for Nos D5515-9 were 3127-3131.

Pilot Scheme Class C/Type 4

EE D200 series (later Class 40)

This was an obvious choice for a Pilot Scheme type, but detailed design was left to EE (EE Contract Number CCF 0874) rather than BR, as with the earlier EE-equipped prototypes. BR knew what it was going to get — basically a company version of No 10203. In fact, EE was turning out an order for 2,000hp diesels for Rhodesia at the time and its design for BR shared a great deal with this export order. The quoted price was £97,090, but this eventually rose to £106,807.

The company's traditional strength underframe approach was used. In consequence recourse was made to the SR design of 1-Co bogie to keep route availability high. A pronounced nose-end housed some equipment and included gangway doors in the outer face for inter-locomotive communication. A clean bodyside was achieved by mounting the engine room air intake grilles at cantrail level.

The inaugural run of the EE D200 series Types 4s was made for invited guests between Liverpool Street and Norwich. No D200 sets off bearing a commemorative headboard. *EE*

The 16SVT Mark II had an EE 822/4C 10-pole main generator, rated at 1,313kW, 1,800A, 730V at 850rpm. Overhung from the main generator was an EE 911/2B 43/48kW auxiliary generator. From new, EE 526/5D 6-pole traction motors were supplied, three per bogie, and connected in three series pairs in parallel across the main generator, being continuously rated at 212hp at a nominal 300V, 600A at 362rpm. The radiator fan was directly driven by a shaft from the free end of the engine. Blue Star multiple-working equipment and sanding gear were included in the locomotive. Livery was standard BR green, with a grey roof and a light grey band between these two colours. As ever, the underframe and bogies were in black, while red was used for the buffer beams and bogie fronts. Numbering was D200-9.

Construction was undertaken at Vulcan and No D200 emerged in March 1958, the first of the Type 4 designs. Acceptance testing was given to Doncaster Works and clearly everything was satisfactory because it was soon at Stratford shed, ready for the inaugural journey on 18 April after a month spent on crew training. The first run was from Liverpool Street to Norwich with a nine-coach load of 335 tons. Several days previously Mr Allen had ridden on a special behind 'Britannia' 7P Pacific No 70039, and his timings of both occasions make an interesting comparison. The 7P had an identical load but was running to a schedule markedly faster than the prevailing norm, so its performance must be judged as a special effort.

A rather attractive GE-pattern signal gantry frames No D203 as it approaches Witham at the head of the 1.45pm Norwich to Liverpool Street train on 7 November 1960.
M. Edwards

No D200 made a faster departure from Liverpool Street, gaining half a minute to Bethnal Green. Climbing Brentwood Bank, both machines made the same time from Romford to the summit, cleared at 53mph. Power on the bank for No D200 was only 1,360rhp, about 200hp less than one would expect, leading to the conclusion that the engine was not quite correctly set. Steam ran faster down to Chelmsford, a general feature of both down and up journeys. By Witham, though, the diesel hung on to its initial advantage. Two slowings for track work then penalised the Type 4 onward to Ipswich. To this point the 7P had bettered even time for the 68.7 miles, whereas No D200 stopped in just under 72 minutes. The 18.3 miles between Mellis and Swainsthorpe took No 70039 13min 55sec with two maxima of 88mph. No D200 occupied 13min 33sec with a full 90mph. On a later footplate run with No D205, the driver used full power over this section, which produced a time of 13min 31sec and the top speed was also 90. This suggests that No D200 was also driven flat out.

In the up direction, diesel beat steam on the stiff ascent to Trowse Upper Junction, but the 7P ran Swainsthorpe to Mellis in 13min 46sec against 15min 02sec for the Type 4, which might not

Initial allocation of the first members of the class was to Stratford for Great Eastern Section duties. On 14 June 1958 No D204 passes Brentwood with the down 'Broadsman'. *Stanley Creer*

have been driven throughout on full power. After Ipswich the diesel made several stops, so further comparison is fruitless, but Mr Allen claimed never to have witnessed a steam effort like it on the GE main line. It is fair to conclude that the new diesel was equal to the Class 7 steam power it was displacing.

The later deliveries from Vulcan went to the East Coast main line and one was diagrammed for a relaunched 'Master Cutler' Pullman service from 15 September 1958, between King's Cross and Sheffield Victoria. This new train replaced the discontinued equivalent that ran out of Marylebone along the former Great Central route, once control of this latter transferred from the ER to the LMR. Mr Allen travelled on the 7.20am Up on the second day behind No D209 with a seven-car 250-ton load.

More than 5 minutes was cut on the 33-minute booking to Retford and the locomotive had time comfortably in hand until south of Peterborough. There were

Below: Coinciding with the arrival of the final examples of the Pilot Scheme batch, the ER re-introduced the 'Master Cutler', but running from Sheffield Victoria to King's Cross rather than Marylebone. An EE Type 4 was rostered for the turn, and No D206 approaches King's Cross with the up service on 7 October 1958. *Brian Morrison*

Right: When brand-new the class was also assigned to the prestigious 'Flying Scotsman' King's Cross-Edinburgh service for a time. No D207 pounds up Holloway bank at the start of the northbound journey on 7 October 1958. *Brian Morrison*

Below right: An interesting aerial study of No 40009 at Buxton depot on 17 October 1981. *Tom Heavyside*

Towards the end of its days, No 40001 stands at Crewe with a freight for Penyfford Quarry.
David N. Clough

easy maxima of 85 descending to the Trent before Newark, and 92 down Stoke bank. Mr Allen was highly impressed with the climb from Arlesey to Stevenage, where the minimum on the 1 in 200 was 75mph. A power calculation suggests that No D209 was also below the predicted output at around 1,400rhp instead of 1,550. Despite signal and permanent way checks, an early arrival was on the cards until a long stop outside the terminus put paid to things. Net time for the 138.6 miles was estimated at 122 minutes, exactly equal to the net schedule.

During 1959 the class averaged 72,321 miles, rising to 111,377 the following year, reflecting long runs on the East Coast line, but decreased to 75,122 during 1961. No D200 remained on the GE Section until 1967, when a move came to Longsight, its last depot before withdrawal in 1981; two years later, however, the locomotive was reinstated at Carlisle Kingmoor and given an overhaul at Toton. No D200 saw regular use on special trains, as well as scheduled passenger services in the North West, before final withdrawal in 1988 when it was presented to the National Railway Museum.

Nos D201-5 also went new to the Great Eastern Section, remaining there until also migrating to the LMR, where they all saw out their days based in the North West. Nos D206-9 went new to Hornsey for East Coast work from King's Cross, the last arriving in September 1958. By 1961 the route had sufficient Type 5 'Deltics' to enable the EE Type 4s to be cascaded to East Anglia to hasten the demise of steam. Like the others, transfer to the LMR came in 1967. Aside from No D200 none survive.

EE produced a solid, workmanlike design in its Pilot Scheme Type 4. Its great bulk helped when hauling (actually stopping) unfitted freights, but it was not well suited to high-speed passenger work. This was because 2,000hp is insufficient to maintain high averages with loads of more than seven coaches, while the traction equipment initially proved unsuited to fast running and flashed over. Engine timing chain failures were a headache that plagued not only this design but also the later Class 50s, and the steam heat generator was also a source of trouble. Once put on to mainly freight or intermediate passenger duties, reliability and availability soared, and the class became (with the EE Type 1 and 3 designs) the best on BR. It was thus a wise gamble to have eventually ordered a total of 200 examples.

EE Type 4	
Length	69ft 6in
Width	9ft
Height	12ft 103/8in
Weight	133 tons
Wheel diameter, powered	3ft 9in
Non-powered	3ft 0in
Engine	EE 16SVT Mk II
Engine output	2,000bhp
Maximum speed	90mph
Tractive effort, maximum	52,000lb
continuous	30,900lb at 18.8mph
Gear ratio	61:19
Fuel tank capacity	730 gallons
Minimum curve radius	4½ chains

EE Rotation Numbers 2367-2376 and Vulcan Foundry Works Numbers D395-D404

NBL D600 series (later Class 41) and Swindon D800 series (later Class 42)

As explained in Chapter 4, the WR felt that it had a strong case for the trial of a diesel-hydraulic transmission system. At the time, though, just about every locomotive builder in the UK had forged an alliance with a manufacturer of electrical equipment, if the builder did not make their own already. NBL, though, already held manufacturing rights for MAN engines and Voith transmissions. It has been said that the BTC refused to grant final approval for the diesel-hydraulic trial until NBL had submitted a formal offer for five locomotives, with a final cost of £102,526. The contract was NBL Locomotive Order QP (Queens Park) 76, while BR Swindon Lot Number 425 was also issued. Up until that point NBL had manufactured few, if any, MAN engines, which were heavier than the Maybach equivalent. Similarly, the Voith transmission was heavier than the Mekydro, and this was always going to make producing a 2,000bhp 80-ton locomotive on a B-B bogie wheel arrangement, as envisaged by the WR, difficult for the company.

In any event, the BTC Mechanical Engineering Department seems to have scuppered this concept in favour of a heavyweight diesel electric alternative, more akin to the battleship-size monsters it had commissioned from BR's own works and EE. Consequently, the WR ended up with a 117-ton machine on A-1-A bogies. Once it appreciated how matters were developing, and not liking the probable result, the WR made a direct approach to Maybach in Germany in the summer of 1955. The outcome was that the WR was

On 30 July 1958 No D601 *Ark Royal* climbs out of Hayle in Cornwall with the 'Cornish Riviera Express'. *P. Q. Treloar*

During the first summer of diesel power on the WR, No D600 *Active* skirts the sea wall near Teignmouth with the up 'CRE'. *K. L. Cook*

convinced that a 2,000bhp locomotive could be built for use in Britain on a B-B bogie arrangement, with overall weight around 80 tons and having a 90mph top speed. Crucially, component manufacture could be carried out here, avoiding the political hurdles of importing a German design so soon after the end of World War 2, at a time when BR's workshops (notably Swindon) were seeing the end of steam locomotive building on the horizon.

Internal BR politics stayed the WR's hand in taking the concept forward until the 'Blue Pullman' sets were under consideration. These were to use high-speed engines and electric transmission in a configuration identical to that of today's HSTs. Piggy-backing on this design, based on quick-running diesels, the WR pushed its proposals again, and in January 1956 received authorisation to build three prototypes at Swindon Works in line with the proven German

V200 concept. The following year the BTC pretty much abandoned the Pilot Scheme by placing further orders for untried designs, and Swindon was given authority to build a further 30 Type 4s, using power trains manufactured by Maybach. Substantial lobbying against this by the British manufacturing industry resulted. Notwithstanding this, in July 1958 NBL secured an order for a further 33 Type 4s but with MAN-Voith power trains/transmissions that had to be manufactured in Britain.

The NBL Type 4s, Nos D600-4, used two MAN L12V18/21BS (L12V18/21A in German) engines rated at 1,000bhp at 1,445rpm. Each engine drove a Voith L306r triple converter transmission through step-up gears. These two power trains were separated by a Spanner train-heating unit. Curiously, the two radiator fans were each driven by an electric motor. The body used a heavy underframe but aluminium side sheets, and cab-end nose-gangway doors were fitted. Multiple-unit coupling was permitted, but only with another D600 series or an NBL D6300, both types being given the Orange Square coupling code. Standard green livery was used with a white line along the solebar between the cab footsteps.

All five received names commemorating Royal Navy warships, which led to the type (and the Swindon-built design) becoming known by that name. Nos D600/1 thus became the first named BR diesels, as well as the first Type 4s. No D600 made its main-line debut on 25 November 1957 on a three-coach test train from South Side CS to Kilmarnock. Between 27 November and 2 December trials with eight coaches were made to Dumfries and on to Gretna Green. It was noted heading for the WR, where it was allocated to Swindon, on 13 January 1958. No D600 entered traffic later that month, followed by No D601 (also to Swindon) in March, and the rest (which went to Newton Abbot) from November.

On 17 February 1958 No D600 worked a special train for invited guests between Paddington and Bristol. Speeds of more than 90mph were attained, but, worryingly, one engine shut down at Badminton on the return leg. The problems encountered with the MAN engines have already been covered in the previous chapter, and unsurprisingly the same issues manifested themselves with the NBL Type 4s. Fortunately their Voith transmissions gave less trouble.

By March No D600 was at work around Swindon, operating as far as Old Oak Common and Gloucester/Cheltenham. In April it gravitated to Plymouth where it was regularly deployed on the 'Cornish Riviera Express' in Cornwall. Meanwhile No D601 was being put through a series of tests with the WR dynamometer car. Among these were tests over the South Devon banks on 15 May, when a 439-ton train was only restarted with difficulty on the steepest gradients, even though the rails were dry. On 16 June No D601 was put into scheduled service on the down 'Riviera', but failed twice in two days and was taken out of traffic.

In 1958 Cecil J. Allen made a footplate run on the down 'Cornish Riviera Express' on No D601, with a load of 410

Examples of NBL passenger prototypes of both Types 2 and 4 in tandem were common on trains over the South Devon banks. In this July 1959 scene, No D6300 appears to be doing all the work, judging by exhaust emissions, with No D601 *Ark Royal* as the train locomotive on the 11.00am Paddington to Plymouth service. *D. S. Fish*

Above: **In June 1960 No D602 is on the last leg of its journey with the up 'Mayflower' from Plymouth as it hurries through Iver.** *Derek Cross*

Above right: **Meanwhile No D601 *Ark Royal* is barely into its stride at Iver with a Paddington to Penzance service on the same day.** *Derek Cross*

Right: **By 17 March 1963 No D603 had acquired a small yellow warning panel on its front end when seen here at Swindon.** *C. P. Boocock*

tons to Westbury and 375 tons thereafter. No fewer than four permanent way slowings between Paddington and Reading prevented the locomotive from showing its paces and caused 4 minutes of lateness. Accelerating from 66 at Maidenhead to 76mph at Twyford suggests 1,575rhp, comparable to an EE Type 4. Climbing the Kennet Valley produced 69mph at Newbury and 77 by Kintbury, 1,680rhp in the same speed range as after Maidenhead. Such solid work saw 3 minutes recovered by the summit at Savernake, passed at 57mph.

No doubt due to prevailing limits, the descent towards the Westbury cut-off line saw nothing higher than 75mph and the slip coach was dropped at Heywood Road Junction just about on time. After Castle Cary No D601 was clearly given its head, with maxima downhill of 86½mph at Charlton Mackrell and 92 at Curry Rivel Junction. Taunton was passed more than

4 minutes early in 131min 38sec at 70mph but, for whatever reason, the climb to Whiteball was disappointing, with a 28mph minimum. It was a similar story ascending the South Devon banks, with Dainton cleared at only 18mph at 1,190rhp, although on Rattery the rhp was better at 1,400 in accelerating from a 21mph minimum to 33 at the summit. These efforts suggest very much lower power for traction when speed was falling against the grade. Nevertheless the train was now more than 4 minutes early and signal checks were, perhaps, inevitable on the run into Plymouth North Road, which was still reached more than 4 minutes up on the 240-minute schedule.

In 1959 the class averaged 72,063 miles, 70,748 in 1960, and 70,622 in 1961. Once sufficient of the D800 production series were in traffic, the D600s were downgraded from express passenger work, primarily because they

were less reliable. The German-built transmission trains did, though, prove less prone to failure than those built by NBL. Based at Plymouth for most of their lives, latterly they were kept in the West Country. In 1967 they migrated to Landore for mineral traffic services until a final return to Plymouth for withdrawal in December 1967.

NBL Type 4

Length	65ft
Width	8ft 8in
Height	12ft 10in
Weight	117 tons
Wheel diameter,	
powered	3ft 7in
non-powered	3ft 3½in
Engines	2 x MAN L12V18/21BS
Engine output	2 x 1,000bhp at 1,445rpm
Maximum speed	90mph
Tractive effort,	
maximum	49,460lb
continuous	39,600lb at 12.6mph
Fuel tank capacity	800 gallons
Minimum curve radius	4½ chains

NBL Progressive Numbers 27660-27664

Meanwhile Swindon was busy designing the three prototype D800s under a January 1956 order that was given Swindon Lot Number 428. This was no easy task because the V200 main components had to be accommodated in a superstructure 10 inches lower and 16 inches narrower than permitted by the German loading gauge. Naturally the work absorbed much time, not least in language translation and conversion from metric to imperial measurements. Inevitably this reflected in the cost per locomotive of £143,645. A stressed-skin superstructure was adopted to keep overall weight down. Using a stressed-skin bodyside as part of the load-bearing arrangement for the body, cut down the size and weight of the underframe. The German K-M bogie was used, which gave satisfactory ride characteristics up to the 75mph limit of the German locomotives; however, it proved rough riding in the UK at 90mph and had to be modified, causing all the D800s to be downgraded to 80mph for a time.

Two Maybach MD650 diesels were used, rated at 1,056bhp (usually quoted as 1,000bhp) at 1,400rpm. Although modified pistons to the later pattern

No D800 *Sir Brian Robertson* poses for the camera inside Swindon Works after being completed on 27 July 1958. The headboard proclaims 'First 2,200hp diesel hydraulic locomotive built in British Railways workshops'. *N. E. Preedy*

Left: **This 1959 photograph of No D800** *Sir Brian Robertson* **captures a typically busy scene at Plymouth North Road, with the 'Warship' on the up 'CRE', and an NBL Type 4 'Warship' alongside.**
N. E. Preedy

Below: **Sonning Cutting was a favourite location for steam photographers but had fallen out of fashion by the 1980s. In this July 1960 view, No D802** *Formidable* **powers westwards at the head of the 'Cornish Riviera Express'.**
Derek Cross

No D802 *Formidable* stands at Bristol Temple Meads. *P. J. Sharpe*

fitted to Nos D803 onwards replaced the original type, engine output was not raised due to the limitation of their lower-input transmissions. Each engine was coupled to a Mekydro K104U hydro-mechanical transmission and mounted at each end of the engine room, separated by the Spanner train-heating boiler. The driver's power handle had six power notches, but this was found to give insufficiently fine control so the production series had a seven-notch controller. For this reason, Nos D800-2 could only multiple among themselves.

No D800 emerged in June 1958, and on 14 July it was named *Sir Brian Robertson* after the BTC Chairman. Subsequent names followed the RN warship theme. All-over standard BR green was applied, with mid-grey for the removable roof panels and the addition of a light grey horizontal band between the cabs. Unusually, tyre sides and wheel hubs were brightly polished, while the buffing gear was red, and black was used for the bogies. The day after being named, No D800 took the down 'Riviera' from Paddington to Plymouth. By October one of the type could be found on the up 'Riviera', then the 6.30pm Paddington to Bristol Temple Meads, before finishing the day by hauling another service to Plymouth. During dynamometer car trials No D801 proved capable of a tractive effort of 48,000lb at 7mph. The trials found a peak transmission efficiency of 82½%.

The Maybach engines were items of precision engineering and required higher standards of maintenance than the more robust medium-speed diesels; however, such attention was not always forthcoming on BR. Nevertheless, even the German-manufactured units suffered failure due to design faults, notably cylinder heads and big-end bearings. Some of the many issues found in the UK were also found in Germany, but certainly not all. There were clearly some fundamental design issues with Maybach engines and these caused significantly higher costs, and reduced locomotive availability, when compared to equivalent diesel-electrics. The Mekydro transmission was also not trouble-free. Sustained efforts by Swindon Works did manage latterly to improve the availability of the Maybach-Mekydro fleet (Class 42 under TOPS) to some 80% in their later years.

Average miles per locomotive during 1959 was very high at 120,402. Regrettably, no performance data for the three prototypes has come to light. On the Bristol road D800s were recorded in the up direction at speeds of 100mph, something their transmission was quite capable of. When the plan to withdraw the whole class was announced in 1967, it was no surprise that Nos D800-2 were the first to succumb, the end coming between August and October 1968.

Swindon Type 4

Length	60ft
Width	8ft 10in
Height	12ft 10½in
Weight	78½ tons
Wheel diameter	3ft 3½in
Engines	2 x Maybach MD650
Engine output	2 x 1,056bhp at 1,400rpm
Max speed	90mph
Tractive effort,	
maximum	48,600lb
continuous	46,900lb at 11.5mph
Fuel tank capacity	800 gallons
Minimum curve radius	4½ chains

BR/Sulzer D1 series (later Class 44)

Despite being fully committed to steam locomotive construction and overhaul, BR's workshops wanted to secure orders for diesel traction. Derby Works had built the LMS prototypes Nos 10000/1 and was a natural choice for the design of machines to form part of the Pilot Scheme. The LMR Mechanical Engineering Department was very keen on the Sulzer engine, much less so on its EE counterpart. The Region also believed that its diesel needs could be met largely from two diesel types: a Class B/Type 2 and a Class C/Type 4. Sulzer's LDA28 engine, in either six- or 12-cylinder configuration, therefore fitted the bill nicely and it was no surprise that these power units were selected for use in the BR designs of Pilot Scheme locomotives.

In designing the Class C under Derby Order D9650, Derby clearly drew on features adopted in both the LMS and Southern prototypes. As before, the body superstructure was not load-bearing, so overall weight was correspondingly greater that it could have been. To keep axle loading down to a figure that would permit a wide route availability, this meant a very long body mounted on 1-Co bogies, mirroring the approach taken by the Southern. Overall weight in working order was more than 133 tons — it is easy to see why the WR was attracted to an 80-ton diesel-hydraulic of similar power. A short nose end was also copied from Nos 10000/1, and incorporated gangway doors for interconnection between locomotives. Bodyside grilles were masked by a long cover unit, and this meant that there were neither windows nor doors along its length. A different design of cover was adopted on the last two, based on an American patented design by Farr Industries and used by General Motors on its 'E' and 'F' Unit diesels.

Sulzer's 12LDA28 diesel was able to produce 2,300bhp at 750rpm in its 'A' form. With Vickers' manufacturing facility not being up and running in time, Sulzer carried out the manufacture of the engines in Switzerland, the main

No D2 *Helvellyn* is pictured brand-new at Derby Works on 30 August 1959 shortly before entry into traffic. *R. A. Panting*

For some reason No D5 *Cross Fell* was making a test run on 8 August 1960 when photographed passing the closed Grayrigg station in the Westmorland fells. *Derek Cross*

generator being shipped there to permit engine testing. Interestingly, BR turned to Crompton Parkinson for supply of the electrical machines. The CP CG426A1 main generator, continuously rated at 1,546/1,531kW, 960/580V, 1610/2640A at 1080rpm, was coupled to the engine output shaft. Auxiliary generator CP CAG252A1, unusually operating at 220V, was overhung from it. Six CP C171B1 traction motors continuously rated at 305hp, 580V, 440A at 450rpm, were mounted on the three innermost axles on each bogie. Control gear was of Allen West manufacture.

Unusually, the radiator fan was driven by a CP electric motor, rather than the (then) customary drive arrangement from a shaft at the free end of the engine. Overall livery was BR green but with mid-

grey for the roof. A 6-inch bodyside stripe and the engine room grille were light grey, with black for the underframes and bogies, but red for the buffer beam. Originally unpainted and therefore polished aluminium, the driver's handrails were later painted white. Running numbers D1-10 were given to the class and the names applied were those of mountains in Northern England and North Wales, explaining why the locomotives were dubbed the 'Peaks'. Construction price turned out to be £142,422, another very high figure.

As built, the performance characteristic was far from ideal for high-speed duties. On No D1's first service run from Derby to St Pancras, the locomotive had to be driven flat out to exceed 70mph, and main generator voltage was noted to be

No D7 *Ingleborough*, on its down
Liverpool service, should have
been attaining more than 80mph at
Welton, south of Rugby, as it races
an Armstrong-Siddeley saloon on
the adjacent empty, de-restricted
M1 motorway on 18 June 1960.
Derek Cross

very high. Initially the field diversion arrangement was modified to give an extra weak field, but eventually it was decided to re-gear the traction motors from 62:17 to 57:22. While this cut the maximum tractive effort from 70,000lb to 55,000lb, it enabled full engine output to be delivered between $8\frac{1}{4}$ mph and $92\frac{1}{2}$mph, a very versatile range for a mixed-traffic machine! In truth, with prevailing freight stock, a maximum tractive effort of 70,000lb was more of a liability than an asset because of the risk of breaking couplings and drawbars. Prior to the re-gearing the high voltages in the motors and main generator when running fast had caused flashovers, and the change in ratio owed as much to dealing with this problem as enhancing speedworthiness.

The class was the last Pilot Scheme order to arrive. No D1 emerged from Derby Works in April 1959 and was displayed at St Pancras station on the 21st. After some initial trials, a naming ceremony as *Scafell Pike* was held at Carlisle Citadel station on 14 July 1959. The locomotive was then allocated to Camden, but spent time at Derby shed until April 1960. The following month saw No D1 move to Longsight until February 1962, when it migrated to its long-term home on the Midland Division, mostly assigned to Toton. A similar pattern of allocation was followed by Nos D2-10, the last not entering service until February 1960. Of the Type 4s, surprisingly this design returned the worst initial performance. Even though predominantly on Class 1 passenger diagrams, in 1960

Just how far north No D7 *Ingleborough* had taken charge of this Perth to Euston train is not known, but it is seen here at Greenholme descending Shap during September 1960.

Derek Cross

the average mileage was a pitiful 35,184, improving to 46,741 in 1961, while availability was only 48%.

Thus the duration of stay on West Coast duties was fleeting, and thereafter the class rarely ventured anywhere close to the mountains after which they were named. In fact, reports during 1960 suggest that about half the class must have been based on the ex-Midland Railway because there were frequent appearances at St Pancras and Manchester Central. For example, No D10 was said to be a regular at the former during March, while in May this locomotive was noted in the company of Nos D2/5. Equally, in November half the type was frequently sighted at Watford Junction. Meanwhile, on 15 June No D3 had arrived into Carlisle on the 9am from

Perth to Euston. After visiting Upperby shed it continued south on a later train.

The reason for the swift downgrading from express passenger to heavy freight in the East Midlands appears to be twofold. First, West Coast electrification was progressing, coupled with the arrival of increasing numbers of EE Type 4s on that route. Second, the next order of BR/Sulzer Type 4s (Class 45) were to be for the former Midland Railway routes from St Pancras to Derby and across country from there to the WR and NER. It seems that the class was deemed non-standard, but could be deployed on the heavy coal workings between Toton Yard and Brent Sidings, north-west London. Ironically, the original lower gearing would have given a better tractive effort characteristic for this utilisation.

No D2 was selected to prove Sulzer's revised rating for its newly developed 'B' series version of the LDA28. This offered 2,500bhp at 750rpm, and it seems that No D2 was selected for trials at the higher power setting. Due to the passage of time the exact events have become lost or blurred, and slightly different versions have appeared in print. One report suggests that No D2's engine seized during initial static testing and this seems to have been a modified 'A' series engine with an intercooler added to make it comparable to the 'B' series. A 'B' series unit, destined for the second batch of BR/Sulzer Type 4s (and therefore built to the enhanced design, rather than purely being uprated), was fitted instead. It does seem a little unlikely that the second series of locomotives was already at an advanced stage of construction in early 1959, to the point where power units had already been delivered to Derby Works. After all, the first locomotive of the second batch, No D11, did not appear for a further 20 months.

This report gives the period of uprating from 19 September 1959 to 25 July 1961, yet the locomotive entered service in May 1959, clearly several months before the modification. A second account states that the return to normal Class 44 output was 23 February 1963. What is also unclear is whether No D2 then received an 'A' series engine at next overhaul, or whether it retained its 'B' series unit. Tantalisingly, in the dying days of the class the survivors were used on several rail tours. While the others were estimated to be producing a 2,300bhp rating, No D2 was clearly more puissant, delivering 2,500bhp.

Perhaps by virtue of the extra power on offer, No D2 was selected for high-speed trials on the West Coast line between Euston and Liverpool in connection with electrification work. For these the higher traction motor gearing was adopted, and on 9 August 1962 110mph was reached with three vehicles. Further trials on 20 June 1964 saw a return to the same route when a seven-car consist was handled at up to 105mph. Comparative braking trials between a Class 9F steam locomotive and No D8 on a 1,000-ton partly fitted coal train demonstrated a better braking effort by the diesel.

Performance data on the 'Peaks' during their early years has proved rather elusive. It is therefore ironic that the only published run that has come to light featured the uprated example, No D2.

Proving that the 'Peaks' were still performing on the West Coast line into 1961, No D7 *Ingleborough* (again!) passes Berkhampstead on 4 November with the up 'Ulster Express' from Liverpool Lime Street. *Peter Beckett*

Above: **On 27 March 1968 No D5** *Cross Fell*, **looking rather shabby, passes Kibworth on a typical mineral train of the period. This was the sort of duty on which the 'Peaks' were to be found from around 1962 until their demise.** *J. H. Cooper-Smith*

Right: **A contrast of original and revised liveries is combined with a rare sighting of the first two 'Peaks' in action together during the summer of 1967. Nos D1** *Scafell Pike* **and D2** *Helvellyn* **approach Barrow-on-Soar on the Midland main line.** *Graham Wignall*

The data seems to have been recorded in early 1960 when the locomotive replaced defective sister No D7 at Derby on a through service from Manchester Central to St Pancras. With a heavy trailing load (for the Midland) of 400 tons, and a 41-minute-late start, the Kentish Town driver had plenty of incentive. The holding of 69mph up the 1 in 200 to Ampthill and a minimum of 63 up the 1 in 200 to Sharnbrook support a 2,500bhp engine rating. Speed reached, but did not exceed, 90mph, and despite a 1-minute call at

Luton, destination was reached in 92min 29sec gross on a 102-minute booking. Mr Allen estimates a net time of 83½ minutes for the 99.1 miles, markedly faster than a Class 7 steam locomotive could achieve.

After overhaul at Derby Works, a running-in trial usually saw the locomotive pilot a Class 45 on a Midland main line service. Emergency rescues also brought unexpected appearances on Class 1 turns. Otherwise the type covered a wide variety of freight duties from Toton, reaching York, Severn Tunnel Junction,

Garston Dock in Liverpool, and Whitemoor Yard, March. Even though scheduled for early withdrawal under the National Traction Plan, due to being deemed non-standard, Class 44 survived until displaced by deliveries of Class 56 to Toton. Nos 44004/8 survive in preservation.

In retrospect this was a design opportunity missed. While aspects of the detailed design were criticised, overall the Derby drawing office should have looked at modern construction techniques to avoid such a bulky product. The bogies were prone to cracking in the same way as the EE Type 4s, though not as badly. Problems also arose with the control gear, while the traction motor flashover issue was never completely resolved. It was regrettable that the design was perpetuated to a total of 193 examples across Classes 44, 45 and 46, when a machine with the same engine and main generator could, and should, have been built into a body mounted on a Co-Co wheel arrangement, weighing in at around 115 tons.

BR/Sulzer Type 4

Length	67ft 11in
Width	9ft 1½in
Height	12ft 10in
Weight	133 tons
Wheel diameter, powered	3ft 9in
non-powered	3ft 0in
Engine	Sulzer 12LDA28A
Engine output	2,300bhp
Maximum speed	90mph
Tractive effort, maximum, original	70,000lb
maximum, revised	50,000lb
continuous, original	41,000lb at 16.5mph
continuous, revised	29,100lb at 23.2mph
Gear ratio, original	62:17
revised	57:22
Fuel tank capacity	840 gallons
Minimum curve radius, original	5 chains
revised	3½ chains

An engineer's train keeps No 44004 busy at Loughborough on 6 July 1975. *Tom Heavyside*

The Chief Officer, Locomotive Construction & Maintenance, of British Railways had not wanted to order a production series of 'Deltic' locomotives, but finally the ER's view prevailed. These were seen as specialist machines and history proved that, once the specialist role was concluded, the running costs for the type outweighed redeployment elsewhere. By 1959 J. F. Harrison had succeeded R. A. Riddles in the Chief Officer post, and was a Sulzer devotee, in preference to the EE SVT engine range.

Like his predecessor, Mr Harrison believed the medium-speed diesel (one with a maximum speed of around 800-900rpm) was the most suitable for rail applications in this country. He was, though, aware of technological improvements that were enabling power per cylinder to be raised, and regarded this as the way to deal with the Regional Operating Departments' calls for greater tractive effort in motive power. With an eye on the need for further large diesels to replace steam during the 1960s, BTC took the prudent step of inviting manufacturers to come forward with prototypes for evaluation. Perhaps encouraged by the willingness on the part of EE to fund *Deltic*, they clearly

Showing the original lime green and brown livery, No D0280 has a light load with the 'Sheffield Pullman' on 6 June 1962, pictured near Potters Bar. *P. J. Sharpe*

After transfer to the WR, No D0280 stands at Swindon on 25 July 1965. Note the revised two-tone green colour scheme. *A. J. Wheeler*

did not see the need for the railway to re-run the Pilot Scheme, under which the latter footed the bill for prototype construction.

On 15 January 1960 the BTC announced that it was seeking a new large Type 4 2,700hp diesel-electric machine, with both steam and electric train-heating capability, and at the same time indicated its desire for a standard design of Type 1 with centre cab. To give some idea of lead times (relevant when looking at the chronology of the large Type 4 project), the Clayton Equipment Company won the Type 1 order on 28 September 1960 and the first of the

Class 17s entered traffic on 19 October 1961. That the 'Claytons' proved unsuccessful is another story. The following sections describe the three designs of large Type 4 that were offered in response to the invitation.

D0280 *Falcon*

Brush had acquired a manufacturing licence for the Maybach engines, possibly with an eye on producing a locomotive with export potential. Prior to acquiring these rights, one of its first ventures into locomotive building had been in 1951 for Ceylon Government Railway. To protect its own export market, Maybach stipulated

On 24 April 1968 the Brush prototype passes Bathampton at the head of an afternoon Bristol Temple Meads to Paddington service. *John C. Sawtell*

that any exports using its engines could not be diesel-hydraulics, leaving Brush with the option of using its own electrical machines, so its intentions were clear. The fast-running Maybachs had the advantage of high power for low weight, something appreciated and demonstrated by EE with *Deltic* — two MD655s only weighed 13.8 tons.

Under Contract No 04/20600, the design of the locomotive that was to become *Falcon*, the name of the Brush works at Loughborough, is reported as having started in 1959, thus in advance of the BTC invitation for a large Type 4. It was to use two Maybach 12-cylinder MD655 engines, rated at 1,400bhp each at 1,500rpm — this was the engine

selected by BR for the large Type 4 diesel-hydraulics being designed and built for the WR. Each engine had a Brush TG 110-56 Mark II main generator rated at 910kW, 1,845A, 493V, or 915kW, 1,500A, 610V, both at 1,500rpm. Each main generator was accompanied by a Brush TG42-20 auxiliary generator, mounted on top of its bigger cousin and driven by a belt arrangement. The six Brush TM 73-68 Mark II traction motors continuously delivered 373hp, 493V, 615A at 704rpm, and employed three stages of field weakening that was predicted to permit full power to be delivered up to the locomotive's 100mph top speed. Each power unit supplied one bogie. The overall weight of the locomotive was 115

The two-tone green paint scheme suited longer locomotive types, including No D0280 *Falcon*. By the date of this picture, 25 March 1968, the machine was based at Bath Road and performing two round trips to Paddington. It is seen here ready to depart from Bristol Temple Meads with the 07.30 up service. *John Chalcraft*

tons, within the stipulated BR axle loading. External styling was interesting in that it differed significantly from previous practice and followed a format that was to be replicated in subsequent classes. The lower part of the cab front was vertical and included a four-character train number indicator box. Above that level were two large windows that sloped inwards slightly. A distinctive lime green and chestnut brown livery was chosen, and running number D0280 was assigned.

The official photographs on completion were taken at Falcon Works on 18 September 1961. On-site testing then took place until 6 October, when the locomotive went to Doncaster Works for acceptance tests. Completion of these on the 13th saw No D0280 make its way up the East Coast line for trial running, working off Finsbury Park. The first revenue trip was on the 16th on the 6.52am King's Cross to Cambridge and 10.5am return. On the 18th it took the 8.15am King's Cross to Hull as far as Doncaster, returning on the 12.20pm ex-Hull. It then took the 8.20pm King's Cross to Edinburgh mail, but suffered a cab heater fire at Hatfield and was returned to Brush for attention.

Returned from repair by the 27th, the diagram to Doncaster resumed, until a trial on the Great Eastern Section between Liverpool Street and Norwich, followed by freight runs from Norwich to

On 16 June 1972 No 1200, now in BR Blue livery, runs into Reading while in charge of the 18.40 Weston super Mare to Paddington train. *G. F. Gillham*

Whitemoor Yard, March. To evaluate the difference between diesel-electric and diesel-hydraulic transmissions, the WR took delivery of the prototype for dynamometer car trials. Thus *Falcon* was delivered to Swindon on 14 December 1961. Prior to the testing, *Falcon* made its Regional passenger debut on the 20th, in the company of brand-new 'Western' class Type 4 No D1000 *Western Enterprise*, working the 6.55am Cheltenham to Paddington train. Among other tests, a 628-ton train was started on the Lickey Incline between Bromsgrove and Blackwell. In doing so a maximum tractive effort of 70,300lb was recorded. Trials with a 'Western' Type 4 diesel-hydraulic, with the same Maybach

engines, measured a maximum tractive effort of 65,500lb, demonstrating that the traditional view by enthusiasts that diesel-hydraulics have more pulling power is wrong. Braking tests with freight stock were conducted descending Lickey. On 13 February *Falcon* reached Plymouth and en route restarted a 576-ton train on the South Devon banks.

With the trials completed, the locomotive returned to Brush for modifications and substitution of the original transfer nameplate for a metal one. Of course the WR had no experience with diesel-electric traction and this may have been why *Falcon* was moved to the ER from April 1962 once trials had been completed. Based at Sheffield Darnall, it

On 14 September 1974 No D1200 *Falcon* shunts wagons at Corporation Road, Newport, on its return to traffic, according to the photographer. *G. Scott-Lowe*

worked the 'Master Cutler' diagrams to King's Cross. Later it spent time on freight movements to Whitemoor Yard with loads of up to 1,800 tons. March to August 1963 were spent back at Loughborough, from where the locomotive appeared in BR Brunswick Green, but with a lighter shade for the solebar. By the end of 1963, 125,000 miles had been run, virtually without incident.

Brush entered into a contract with BR for the hire of the locomotive at £8,750 per annum, subject to a minimum mileage of 80,000. Brush was to maintain the electrical equipment as part of the deal. Following overhaul at Loughborough, *Falcon* went to Swindon in January 1965 to have AWS fitted. The WR

had now begun to receive allocations of diesel-electric traction, so No D0280 would no longer be unique. The following month *Falcon* was allocated to Bristol Bath Road, from where it worked two return trips to Paddington each day. One example of such a schedule encompassed the 9.15am and 5.15pm from Bristol and the 1.45pm and 10pm ex-Paddington, the latter being the Penzance postal.

After only two months, engine and cooling system defects led to the decision to send the locomotive to Swindon for a top-end overhaul of its Maybach engines, as well as a full overhaul of the cooling system. Attention was given to the train-heating boiler, and the water scoop for refilling this was removed. Although back

A sad end for a successful prototype: No D1200 meets its fate in Cashmore's Yard, Newport, on 28 March 1976. *Tom Heavyside*

in traffic in August, in September No 2 engine suffered two failures due to cracked cylinder blocks and in December three cylinder heads cracked. Suspicion fell on a failure to adhere properly to Maybach's maintenance schedules, which would certainly not have happened while Brush had responsibility. All these troubles meant that only 29,400 miles were run during 1965.

During 1966 a further 92 days were lost due to engine defects, suggesting that Swindon accorded such repairs low priority — 57,500 miles were covered. The following year was even less productive, with 144 days on the sidelines, of which 61 were due to the steam heating boiler controls burning out, but 1968 was more productive, *Falcon* covering 90,400 miles. The failure rate was, though, a poor 7,500 miles per

casualty. In July 1968 O. S. Nock timed a run from Paddington to Swindon, and with a late departure there was an incentive for time recovery. With an 11-coach 410-ton load, Southall was passed in 10min 02sec. Acceleration continued to the 90mph line limit by Slough and this was held to Maidenhead, falling to 87mph at Twyford. Reading was reached in 30min 05sec for the 36 miles, which, while creditable, was regularly surpassed by Class 50 in later years. The succeeding 41.3 miles to Swindon occupied 34min 47sec, speed being sustained at 81½mph between Wantage Road and Shrivenham against the slight grade.

Falcon was not fitted with train air braking equipment whereas the new Mark 2 coaching stock, which required such a system, was coming into service. There was insufficient room to add air brake cylinders as well as the existing vacuum exhausters, so consideration was given to withdrawing the locomotive; however, it was purchased from Brush instead and given a fresh lease of life. The agreed price was £20,000, while the braking system modifications and an overhaul cost a further £43,000, more than half the price of a brand-new Class 50. Sanction for these developments came in April 1970 and took until December to complete. It is somewhat surprising that *Falcon* was kept, because the National Traction Plan had decided to prune the locomotive fleet of non-standard types, and clearly *Falcon* was unique, albeit with engines and traction motors in use in other WR classes. No D0280 emerged in all-over blue, renumbered No D1200 and classified Class 53, and was (for the time) unusual in being able to operate only air-braked trains. It entered capital stock as a BR locomotive on 19 December 1970.

On release from the works the locomotive was used for a series of trials on various WR routes, the purpose of which is not known. By mid-1971 *Falcon* was back on passenger duty at Bristol until July or August 1972, when it was transferred to Ebbw Junction depot for freight use. By then the WR was receiving new Mark 2 stock that required electric heating, and No D1200 lacked this facility, hence a move away from passenger work. Annual mileages now dropped to around 40,000. Ebbw Junction was an odd choice of base for a machine with Maybach engines because the depot had no experience of them. Perhaps because of this two months later it migrated to Cardiff Canton, reportedly hauling freightliners. In May 1973, however, it returned to end its days at Ebbw Junction. Further, the duties assigned were unfitted transfer freights between Alexander Dock, Newport and East Usk Yard, on which a Type 2 was normal power.

In 1974 *Falcon* was sent to Loughborough for attention in Brush's works. Nobody seems to have been aware that Falcon Works was no longer rail-connected, so the locomotive returned to South Wales.

On 27 June 1975 *Falcon* was due a 'B' exam and one of the traction motor bearings was running hot. Instead of spending money on it, the locomotive was put into store and withdrawn on 5 October. It had run 550,000 miles since 1961, 40,000 miles annually. Cashmore bought the vehicle for £5,125 for scrap. The weak spot in the design proved to be the engines, whose six-valve cylinder head was prone to fracture. Unlike with the WR diesel-hydraulics with the same engine, *Falcon's* were special because of the generator mounting plate and the Woodward governor to suit the electric transmission. Lessons learned were incorporated in the near-concurrent design work on the BR/Brush Type 4 (Class 47). *Falcon* had a very good theoretical characteristic: full engine output was available between 11 and 100mph, a much wider range than any other Type 4 of either diesel-electric or diesel-hydraulic configuration. While the continuous rating speed was a little high at 28½mph, the rail horsepower of 2,160 was better than the equivalent diesel-hydraulic.

D0280 *Falcon*	
Length	68ft 10in
Width	8ft 10¾in
Height	12ft 10in
Weight	115 tons
Wheel diameter	3ft 7in
Engines	2 x Maybach MD655
Engine output	2,800bhp
Maximum speed	100mph
Tractive effort, maximum	60,000lb
continuous	28,500lb at 28.5mph
Gear ratio	60:19
Fuel tank capacity	1,400 gallons
Minimum curve radius	4 chains

Works Number 280 of 1961

Above: **On 14 May 1962 No DP2 passes Runcorn while heading for Edge Hill from Crewe, possibly during crew training and shortly before entering service.** *E. N. Bellass*

Right: **This July 1962 official illustration is taken on the LMR, with No DP2 heading for Euston.** *EE*

DP2

Except for those few that were involved at the time, or have since studied the subject, the amount of funding allocated by EE to development of new diesel engines during the 1950s was substantial. Consideration of the different projects falls outside the scope of this book, but what is important to appreciate is that neither the RK nor the SVT ranges of engine were selected for major development; their budgets were quite small. Hopes pinned on other engines proved ill-founded when insurmountable technical problems caused their abandonment.

When in January 1959 the BTC ordered from EE a new medium-power locomotive (later Class 37) of a new power classification, Type 3 — which had not been envisaged under the Pilot Scheme — the engine to be used was a charge-cooled version of the Mark II SVT

(designated CSVT — Charge-cooled, Supercharged, Vee-cylinder arrangement, Traction application). The output per cylinder was pushed up from 125hp to 167hp, and in 12-cylinder form this offered 2,025hp. In the event, the BTC asked for a rating of no more than 1,750hp.

It was not until 25 May 1961 that EE unveiled its 16-cylinder version of the CSVT, offering 2,700hp at 167hp per cylinder. This was always a big, robust but crude prime mover, unlike its Sulzer counterpart.

Just when the DP2 project got started is not known. Clearly the company's announcement that the development of a 16CSVT engine had passed proving trials indicates that matters were under way by May 1961 to offer a design that met the BTC's call for a new Type 4. Obviously, though, the DP2 project must have been sanctioned well before then. Again, to be fair, EE was preoccupied in producing the Class 55 'Deltics', as well as other main-line orders for home and overseas. It was also road testing its gas turbine prototype, GT3. Nevertheless, it was a very big company, with more works facilities than any other private locomotive builder.

EE clearly had to throw its hat into the new Type 4 ring, and time was running out for its new diesel engines undergoing development. Contract No CCM 2029 was raised for the work. The cheapest and most expeditious option was to use the jigs employed to build a production series 'Deltic' bodyshell to accommodate the new 16CSVT engine. Speculation has it that what should have been D9017 became DP2. In truth there are fundamental differences between DP2's body and that of the production 'Deltics'. The actual D9017 entered service in November 1961, so, working back, construction of DP2 would have started in early summer, around the time that the 2,700hp 16CSVT became available. This helps to establish a milestone in the DP2 project.

Really DP2 was little more than a demonstrator for the 16CSVT, set to deliver 167hp per cylinder, roughly

2,700hp in total. Although EE had already sold the BTC the intercooled version of this engine, as fitted to Class 37, it was only rated at 146hp per cylinder at the latter's request. The 167hp-per-cylinder rating had, however, already been used in overseas orders. EE had been secretive about the engine development work it had been carrying out, unlike Sulzer, which had invited the BTC to view progress on enhancing the LDA diesel. Naturally this did not help in persuading the BTC that the large leap in output for the 16-cylinder version from 2,000hp (as in Class 40) to 2,700hp (as offered for the proposed new standard BTC Type 4) was not going to bring problems.

As noted above, the uprating work on the 16CSVT had been done almost on the cheap because the bulk of the development budget was being spent on other diesel engine projects. Hence a full redesign had not taken place. Notable here was the continued use of a chain drive for the camshafts, rather than the use of gears as found on the Sulzer equivalent. Internal politics within EE delayed this full redesign for a decade because the rail traction and industrial divisions bickered over footing the cost. Eventually the Mark III version did emerge around 1971 and was fitted in both Class 56 (in 16-cylinder form) and Class 58 (in 12-cylinder form). If only this bickering had been dealt with earlier and EE had devoted more effort to the successful SVT Mark II unit, and not been so secretive, Sulzer would have faced stiffer competition and the BTC/Brush new standard Type 4 (the D1500s or Class 47) might not have been multiplied to 512 locomotives.

Using an extra set of mechanical components from the production run of the 'Deltics' cut down EE's build costs for DP2. Hence most of the superstructure, cab layout and bogies were identical. However, within the engine room the arrangement was more akin to a Class 37, because one large engine and generator set was fitted instead of two smaller ones. The radiators and radiator fan were located at the free end of the engine, and shutters were fitted in the bodyside to provide an air flow for cooling purposes. These shutters were thermostatically controlled, unlike on Class 37. The weight in working order was 105 tons, 6 tons heavier than a Class 55 but slightly lighter than a Class 37.

The close similarity to these classes helped DP2 win favour with the operating department because driver training was minimal. The external styling did not, however, conform to the BTC's new thinking, which required a flat cab front. Although a steam heating boiler for the train was fitted, no provision for an electric train supply was made, although this had been a requirement within the BTC outline for its new standard Type 4. The maximum design speed was quoted as 105mph, though in service this was (initially at least) limited to 90mph.

A drab all-over dark green livery was used initially, revised later to two-tone 'Deltic' green. While the Brush prototype *Falcon* and the BRCW prototype *Lion* both received numbers, DP2 did not. The story of why it did not bear a name has been told before, but for the record EE planned to use *Enterprise*, but this was bestowed on the new WR Type 4 D1000. When *Challenger* was suggested, an EE director called a halt to the naming process, saying that the other prototypes were the 'challengers'. Instead, the internal working name of Diesel Prototype 2, in abbreviated form, was used.

In summary, DP2 used pretty much off-the-shelf components to trial the 16CSVT engine in service. Only the 12-pole EE 8401/B main generator was new. It is therefore really doubtful whether the locomotive can truly be called a prototype because there was virtually nothing 'new' in it; it was largely an assembly of established engineering brought together for the first time.

On 2 April 1962 Mr F. G. Manning, the BTC contracts manager, wrote to EE at its Stafford office to offer terms for DP2's use on BR. After an inspection by the railway's engineers, the locomotive was to be used for an initial six-month period from the date it was delivered to the BTC;

From July 1963 the EE prototype moved to the ER, where it covered a Type 5 'Deltic' diagram until the end of the Summer timetable. Like so many of its ilk, the pioneer was then deployed on the 'Sheffield Pullman' turn, and this interesting study was taken in October 1963 at the site of Little Bytham station.
J. S. Hancock

this period would then be extended until either party gave a month's notice of termination. The BTC was to supply footplate staff, who were to be trained by EE. Additional skilled assistance was to be provided by EE as judged appropriate by the BTC.

Routine external cleaning, examinations and external maintenance were down to the BTC, which would supply its own spares, if these were stock items. EE had to supply free of charge any non-stock items, while also being responsible for all other maintenance. Either party could withdraw DP2 for modification at any time, subject to reasonable notice. If the frequency of such modifications or general unreliability became unacceptable to the BTC, it would terminate the agreement. Fortunately for historians, detailed records were to be kept of duties performed, consumables used and faults and failures.

On 2 May 1962 DP2 made a proving trip from Vulcan Foundry, where it was built, to Chester and back. This was to check instrumentation and general fitness to run. After some tests and adjustments at Vulcan and Crewe, on the 8th it took a 475-ton test train from Crewe to Penrith and back. Passing Tebay at 80mph, Shap summit was breasted at 43mph. Three days later crew training between Euston and Birmingham began off Camden shed and entry into revenue service followed on the 14th.

The initial diagram covered had previously been used in part for evaluating Stanier's 'Turbomotive' and DP1, *Deltic*. It comprised the 7.45am Euston to Liverpool, 2.5pm return, 7.15pm Euston-Perth as far as Crewe, and 12.30am parcels on the return. This six-day diagram involved 3,800 miles per week and left Sunday for maintenance. Of course West Coast upgrading and

This striking official photograph sees No DP2 departing from King's Cross with a Cambridge service. *EE*

electrification work was under way and, coupled with schedules being based around the 2,000hp Class 40, timings were not taxing for so powerful a machine as DP2. During tests between Euston and Crewe, a 3-hour journey, only 27 minutes were spent on full power. Other trials between Euston and Glasgow revealed only a modest load factor that fluctuated with train schedule and load as follows:

'Caledonian'	315 tons	55.3%
'Midday Scot'	430 tons	65.3%
'Night sleeper'	510 tons	64%

The average power requirement for the 'Midday Scot' was 1,775hp, and 1,500hp for the 'Caledonian'.

During this initial phase several derailments occurred. The most serious came on 19 May when DP2 had the honour to be the first locomotive to enter a new diesel shed built at Camden. To assist servicing, the rails were raised 3 feet above floor level, but these splayed when DP2 ran on to them and it dropped 14 inches. Fortunately only minor damage was suffered.

From the Winter timetable DP2 moved to a Euston-Carlisle diagram, involving the 1.25pm down and 1.25am up, which accumulated a similar weekly mileage. Demonstrating how much it had in hand on prevailing timings, one day it ran over platelayers' tools near Tamworth, causing a 12-minute delay for examination. Despite this, Euston was reached 14 minutes early, a gain of 26 minutes! Possibly its first on-line failure was during January 1963. On a very cold night the train was stopped for 30 minutes south of Crewe and the radiators froze, causing the engine to shut down. Although no serious damage occurred, DP2 had to be removed from its train.

From the Summer 1963 timetable, starting on 6 May, came a fresh set of turns, this time to Blackpool on the 5.5pm down and 8am up. By June tyre turning was needed, so DP2 returned to Vulcan for the work to be done, together with a 5,000-hour engine exam. In the 13 months since entry into traffic, 164,600 miles had been run and 4,500 engine hours clocked. Judged against the standards of the day, this was a spectacular demonstration of reliable running, because no other traction unit would have approached this level of use. During the examination at Vulcan no engine components needed replacing, but the Mark II version of the Clayton train-heating boiler was installed.

Several factors may have brought DP2's move to the ER when Vulcan finished its overhaul in July 1963. Clearly the LMR was not going to be a major user of diesel traction once West Coast electrification was finished. Better therefore to let the ER have an opportunity to evaluate its potential, just as EE had done with *Deltic* to good effect. The ER had schedules that were more demanding, so potentially offered a better test. Finally, EE was under contract to maintain the Class 55 fleet and these were having to come out of traffic at that time for modifications to the train-heating boiler. Slotting DP2 into a gap in the Class 55 pool would assist the company.

Now based at the new Finsbury Park depot, DP2 worked to Leeds and back on 13 July before taking up King's Cross 'Deltic' No 7 diagram from the 15th. This encompassed the following:

Of course, prevailing speed limits on the East Coast route did not fully stretch the production 'Deltics', so the lower power of DP2 was not really an issue.

With the end of the Summer timetable, and the need to deputise for Class 55 gone, DP2 began to work to Leeds. It returned on the up 'Yorkshire Pullman', then did a return trip from King's Cross to Grantham, 583 miles daily. Since arriving on the ER and before going for works attention, DP2 achieved 100% availability. In October 1963 O. S. Nock made a footplate trip from Leeds to the capital on the Pullman with a trailing load of 441 tons tare, 460 tons gross. The driver and secondman were from Leeds Copley Hill shed. Full power on the rising grades around 1 in 200 between Doncaster and Retford brought a balancing speed of around 69mph. This approximates to 2,200rhp, an extremely good figure, and resulted in an actual time of less than 20 minutes, against 20½ booked, despite a signal and permanent way check.

Running several minutes early, further signal checks intervened at Grantham, with speed down to 15mph. Recovery up the 1 in 200 to Stoke was to 60mph, followed by 90mph on the descent to Peterborough, this being the top speed permitted at the time. A succession of signal checks interrupted the progress and spoiled the climb to Stevenage, with

DP2 diagram, Summer 1963

Day	Depart	Arrive
Sunday		King's Cross 6am
	Maintenance	
	King's Cross 5.10pm	Newcastle 10.50pm
Monday	Newcastle 12.47am	King's Cross 5.24am
	King's Cross 10.10am	Edinburgh 4.30pm
	Edinburgh 10.30pm	
Tuesday to Friday		King's Cross 5.24am
	King's Cross 10.10am	Edinburgh 4.30pm
	Edinburgh 10.30pm	
Saturday	King's Cross 10.10am	Edinburgh 4.30pm
	Edinburgh 10.05pm	

local maxima of 84 at Sandy and Three Counties. A locomotive failure at King's Cross then prevented an arrival ahead of time, causing DP2 to wait for a platform.

Soon after this run came the opportunity to send DP2 to the Darlington works of Robert Stephenson & Hawthorns (part of EE) for new bogies of a cast steel pattern, replicating a similar change to the production 'Deltics'. Now DP2 was used on the 'Master Cutler' from Sheffield to King's Cross comprising two daily round trips and crewed from Sheffield Darnall shed. This was a lightly loaded train of between seven and nine vehicles and timed for a Type 3, on which as little as 20 minutes on full load was called for by DP2.

Cecil J. Allen made a return footplate run from London to Sheffield in March 1964. As on Mr Nock's journey, the performance was marred by the number of interruptions to the running. For this reason an assessment of power is not possible, though operation of the third stage of field weakening at 62mph suggests that the diesel was possibly not producing full rating. Both footplate commentators spoke very highly of the locomotive's capabilities and smooth ride. Mr Allen compared DP2's journey with a contemporary trip behind BR/Brush Type 4 No D1509. The latter had a load one coach heavier and had the honours, being clearly more powerful.

After exhibition at Marylebone in April 1965, DP2 entered Vulcan for overhaul, having completed 380,000 service miles in roughly three years. From 2 April, under a supplemental agreement to that of April 1962 between the British Railways Board and EE, the former agreed to pay a hire charge for DP2's services. A rate of 2s 6d per mile, backdated to 8 September 1963 (presumably when it ceased to be EE's stand-in for Class 55s under repair) was agreed. It was, though, subject to a minimum annual fee of £16,250, while for miles above 150,000 annually the rate dropped to 2 shillings.

DP2 emerged from Vulcan in the standard Class 55 two-tone green, and from 14 June was allocated to Tinsley depot, Sheffield, appearing on turn 60 Monday to Friday, with part of Finsbury Park's turn 22 on Saturday. It now made two return trips on weekdays from Sheffield to King's Cross, the last on the 11.20pm Tinsley to King's Cross goods, with a return run from the capital to Doncaster on Saturdays. On 13 August, however, there was a re-allocation back to Finsbury Park, although the trains worked were the same.

DP2's worthiness finally proved itself when, in 1965, British Rail ordered 50 Type 4s of a new design from EE. These were to have the same engine and main generator set and bogies as DP2, but the similarity virtually ended there. Within BR, the new Railway Technical Centre at Derby wanted a more modern design than its current standard Type 4, the Class 47, and specified an electronic control system. DP2 was taken out of service on 31 January 1966 and sent to Vulcan for a 3,000-hour engine exam together with installation of such a control system.

EE had been trialling electronic power control on a handful of Class 37s at Stratford. It had refined a static field amplifier unit for the main generator (dubbed a KV10 by EE) and this made possible very precise control of power output. The BRB Chief Engineer (Traction & Rolling Stock) wanted electronic control within the new Class 50 design, and DP2 was an obvious choice of locomotive in which to carry out trials. Having entered the works on 31 January 1966 for both the electronics to be fitted and also the 3,000-hour exam, it was some time before EE felt able to release the locomotive into traffic.

On 6 June a test run was made from Newton-le-Willows to Chester and back. Two days later came a loaded trial from Vulcan to Carlisle with a 16-coach, 500-ton train. During the test a stop was made at Scout Green on Shap. Restarting on the 1 in 75, 30mph had been attained by the summit. The equipment installed now featured a separate control whereby the main generator current could be preset

After overhaul and repaint into 'Deltic' livery, No DP2 pauses at York with the Edinburgh to King's Cross car carrier. *Ian Allan Library*

by the driver to any desired level between minimum and maximum to suit prevailing adhesion conditions. The purpose of this was to assist when rail conditions were poor and wheelslip likely, and was a more precise arrangement for limiting power than the driver's power controller. Under normal rail adhesion conditions electronic control was quicker-acting than a conventional control system, but otherwise offered no appreciable benefit to the driver.

On 14 June DP2 made its way back to the ER, stabling overnight at Cricklewood. In an internal memo dated 20 June the ER General Manager gave instructions for it to be kept on high-mileage turns. From the 20th it took up Clarence Yard 27 diagram on Tuesdays to Saturdays and Gateshead 16 diagram on Mondays. These involved hauling the car carrier between Holloway and Edinburgh and return, while on Saturday there was a round trip to Doncaster. Maintenance was, as previously, to be carried out on Sunday.

August proved to be a bad month, starting with a derailment at Edinburgh on the 4th. Two main generator flashovers were reported on successive days after release from repair at Doncaster on the 24th, the first of which caused removal from the down car carrier at Peterborough on the 28th. The flashovers were attributed to loose brushgear in two traction motors on the temporary 'Deltic' bogies fitted while DP2's were being repaired; the latter were refitted on 24 September. The end of the Summer timetable meant that the car carrier diagram finished, and during October DP2 was to be found on King's Cross to Cambridge duties.

Further prototype testing of features to be used in the new Class 50 saw EE engineers install additional kit in DP2 during mid-November. The work was done at Finsbury Park depot and creep trials of the slow-speed control system were made there on the 15th. Next day DP2 was put on a rake of wagons in Ferme Park yard. On the 17th the other new item of equipment, an electronic automatic voltage regulator, was tested when the locomotive was back on the 09.05 King's Cross to Cambridge service.

Neither BR nor EE were happy with the low miles being run. A memo from the

General Manager, again to his North Eastern and Scottish counterparts on 20 December, said that to honour the agreement with EE, a month's trial was scheduled from 2 January 1967 on the Clarence Yard Number 6 Type 5 'Deltic' diagram. This took the 12.00 down to Edinburgh and the 22.30 back, 4,500 miles per week. Prior to this some time was spent on a diagram to Leeds. The trial on the 'Deltic' diagram was deemed successful and was extended for a further month. For the remainder of its operating life the trains covered by this diagram (which took in a trip to Leeds) became the regular work. The same memo from the General Manager confirms that DP2 continued to be accompanied by an EE technician when in service.

Meanwhile the November trials of the slow-speed control equipment had not been satisfactory, partly due to equipment problems, and also the conditions in Ferme Park yard. EE was granted further trials, this time in the Doncaster area on 28 January. Using the new electronics, which EE had fitted at Doncaster Works, a train of 38 wagons and two brake-vans grossing 1,648 tons was provided for proving purposes. One of the lines out of Doncaster towards Goole was selected as the test site and the conditions were wet. Although DP2 had sanding gear, this was not used.

The new slow-speed control system performed better and the prevailing rail conditions also afforded a test of the electronic control system. On a rising 1 in 200 gradient DP2 struggled to get on the move due to repeated wheelslip. Using the new current-limiting potentiometer, or tractive effort control, the tendency to slip was reduced, while the electronics were able to arrest wheelslip very rapidly. More trials were held later at Finsbury Park.

Returning to London on 29 January, maintenance and further experimental modifications occupied two more days before a return to traffic on 1 February on the 12.00 to Edinburgh. Published runs on this train prove that DP2 could keep the schedule and run up to 100mph, despite a typical 12-car load. During a Newcastle to Edinburgh journey, published by Cecil J. Allen in 1967, it is clear that the full rated output of 2,700bhp was being developed.

Over the succeeding months different legs of Clarence Yard 6 diagram were worked, as well as the 10.10 down. On 31 July DP2 was heading north of York on its booked turn when it collided with derailed cement wagons. The resulting damage was severe and it came off the ER's locomotive allocation on 9 September.

EE considered repairing the damage and as late as 1968 memos record plans to move DP2 to Doncaster for the work to be done. Eventually the proposal was abandoned, and it languished at Vulcan until 1970, when it was cannibalised, with components going into the Class 50 pool. Its 16SVT engine initially went into Class 50 No 417 and finally finished its days in No 50037, where it suffered a major failure in September 1991, causing its current host to be withdrawn. The power unit's final resting place was dumped in No 50023.

DP2 accumulated 607,300 miles in just over five years. This was a remarkable figure, probably surpassed only by the 'Deltics' during the 1960s. Between 20 June 1966 (after modifications at Vulcan) and 31 July 1967, DP2 covered 170,415 miles. Excluding on-depot failures, because no information is available whether this delayed the booked train, nine failures on the road have been traced. This gives 19,000 miles per casualty, appreciably better than either a 'Deltic' or Class 50.

A further factor in its favour was that maintenance was thorough and not skimped. Regular checks were made by EE staff to look for potential problems. Having an EE riding technician obviously also aided in dealing with faults encountered while on the road. Its success as a prototype was due to virtually all its components being already in service in other locomotives. What has not been explained, however, is why its main generator gave so little trouble, whereas the same machines in both Class 50 and Portugal's 1800 Class suffered failures.

DP2

Length	69ft 6in
Width	8ft 9½in
Height	12ft 10in
Weight	105 tons
Wheel diameter	3ft 7in
Engine	EE 16CSVT Mk II
Engine output	2,700bhp
Maximum design speed	105 mph
Tractive effort, maximum	55,000lb
continuous	36,000lb at 21.5mph
Gear ratio	53:18
Fuel tank capacity	900 gallons
Minimum curve radius	4 chains

EE Rotation Number 3205 and Vulcan
Foundry Works Number D733

D0260 *Lion*

As discussed in the section about *Falcon*, by the late 1950s the BR's Chief Officer, Locomotive Construction & Maintenance, had pretty much decided that he preferred Sulzer to EE engines. This was despite the comparable engines costing £45,000 and £26,000 respectively. There was also quite a difference in weight, 22.3 tons as opposed to 19.4. Sulzer's LDA28 unit was delivering 208bhp per cylinder in 'B' form, as used in the BR and BRCW Type 2s and BR Type 4s. With technical modifications to the intercooling system and a rise in maximum speed from 750rpm to 800rpm, the company felt confident to rate its LDA28 in 12-cylinder arrangement at 2,750bhp, 229hp per cylinder in 'C' form.

Again, timing is unclear, but it seems likely that the *Lion* project was a direct response to the BTC invitation of January 1960, and it was discussed at a meeting held at BTC headquarters on 4 November 1960. The engine manufacturer became aware that Brush was designing *Falcon* with two Maybach engines as its response, and sought a partner with which to collaborate to produce a 2,750bhp Co-Co locomotive. Its approach to BRCW, with which it had collaborated on building the Type 2 designs, met with interest. Associated Electrical Industries, recently formed as a result of the merger of BTH and Metrovick, agreed to join the

No D0260 *Lion* was first deployed on Paddington to Wolverhampton Low Level passenger services, and shedded at Wolverhampton Stafford Road. After arrival from London, it appears to be being uncoupled, ready to make way for 'Castle' class No 5031 *Totnes Castle*. *Ian Allan Library*

Lion's driving position, showing three ammeters, one for each pair of traction motors, rather than a single ammeter for main generator current. The speedometer records only up to 100mph.

David N. Clough collection

consortium as supplier of the electrical machines.

The task was substantial because of the need to produce a Co-Co wheel arrangement with a 19-ton maximum axle load. Weight was saved in all aspects of the construction of the body; for example, the relatively new practice of employing a stressed body skin that was load bearing kept weight down. Fluting of the mild steel plates below waist level was a novel touch to enhance appearance, and probably also increased strength in compression as with Classes 66 and 67. Extensive use was made of asbestos for bodyside insulation. The engine compartment roof panels were of fibreglass and could be opened by 6 inches to allow hot air to escape before maintenance. Adjacent to these panels were oil-wetted filters to supply clean air to the engine compartment. Unusually, the radiators were also mounted at roof level.

BTH was the British arm of Thomson-Houston, with Alsthom its French counterpart. By virtue of this, the bogie was of an Alsthom design that featured twin rubber-cone body support pivots and radius-arm-guided axle boxes. The bogie frame was of fabricated mild steel.

The generator group consisted of three machines: train-heating, traction and auxiliary; arranged in tandem, these were direct-driven from the engine output

shaft. An AEI TG5303 main generator was fitted, continuously rated at 496/780V, 3,500/2,245A, 1,736/1,751kW, both at 1,150rpm. An AEI AG.106 train-heat generator, with a continuous rating of 800V, 480A, 384kW at 690/1,150rpm was installed. The auxiliary generator was an AEI AG.105. Six AEI Type 253 traction motors were axle-hung, nose-suspended on each bogie axle. Continuously rated at 355hp, 495V, 585A at 790rpm on full field, these were an existing design for narrow-gauge railways and in consequence were relatively small. These motors were also used in the standard BR Type 2 1,250bhp locomotive (later Class 25), which was ordered at the same time. Motor gearing permitted a 100mph top speed.

The control system replicated that used in the BR/Sulzer Type 2s that had BTH switchgear. Certain modifications were needed, not least because of the addition of electric train-heating equipment. The driver's power handle was marked 'Off', 'Full' and 'Top'; the latter position cut off train heating to give extra power for traction. If train heating was not being supplied, engine rpm was increased to its maximum. Unusually, the driver's instruments used ultra-violet illumination. Ammeters recorded motor current, rather than the usual British practice of main generator current.

The locomotive was finished in a striking, if utterly impractical, white livery. At 114 tons in working order, it was slightly lighter than *Falcon*, but was within the stipulated 19-ton axle load limit. *Lion* was actually the most powerful (just!) single-unit diesel locomotive in the world at the time, being the first rail application of the 'C' variant of the 12LDA28 engine running at 2,750bhp. During the first half of May (the date has not been traced) D0260 (the BR running number) was exhibited at Marylebone station, one of many such appearances for new locomotives. On the 14th of that month, service running on the WR Paddington to Birmingham Snow Hill route commenced. Three days later the main generator flashed over while

After transfer to the ER, *Lion* was used on the 'Yorkshire Pullman' and 'Sheffield Pullman' services, and these three scenes depict the former. Left shows the Pullman at Copley Hill on the approach to Leeds. Having arrived at Leeds Central, below sees the locomotive shunting the Bradford portion on to the Harrogate portion. The bottom photograph was taken at Tingley, south of Leeds. *All Eric Treacy*

heading north at Southam Road & Harbury, south of Leamington Spa; the cause was a fuse on the train heat generator voltmeter that had been wired across, thus offering no protection.

Lion resumed activities on the Birmingham road on the 25th, apparently based at Wolverhampton Stafford Road shed, sensibly close to BRCW's Smethwick plant. Mr Allen published a log in the August 1962 issue of *Modern Railways* from C. R. Weaver on the 7.25am ex-Wolverhampton. Delays to trains because of engineering work or signals have been the bane of train running during the early years of the present decade, and one forgets how bad such delays were during the 1950s and 1960s. Between Leamington Spa and Paddington No D0260 suffered

seven checks and three dead stands due to signals. The trailing load was 11 cars weighing 420 tons gross, and the net time for the 87.35 miles was around 81 minutes. As with No D0280's run quoted above, there is insufficient data for power output assessment. Of note, though, were maxima of 103mph after Bicester and 105 after Gerrards Cross, remarkable for a diesel in that era, excepting the East Coast 'Deltics'.

After several weeks of express passenger duties, including round trips between Paddington and Swindon, the locomotive was put through a series of dynamometer car trials between 24 July and 15 August. These included restarting a 569-ton train on the steepest sections of the South Devon banks, followed by restarting a 19-coach 635-ton load up the Lickey Incline. During the latter the main generator was described as sparking like a Catherine wheel! This was due to a technical fault that was rectified.

D0260 was returned to BRCW for attention to a number of issues that had emerged during the trials, not reappearing until March 1963. Further trial running took place during August between Birmingham and High Wycombe and again on the Lickey. This time a 20-coach load was restarted without main generator sparking, even with 6,000A of current. On 9 September *Lion* was transferred to the ER, based at King's Cross, from where it worked the 'Yorkshire Pullman' until suffering a control cubicle fault. Put back into service on the 'Sheffield Pullman', while working this service on 20 January 1964 another main generator flashover occurred, this time at Huntingdon, though it did complete its journey.

A further problem was a serious leak in the engine sump, resulting in the loss of 20 gallons of lubrication oil each day. Several leaks had also manifested themselves in the water system. Return to BRCW coincided with the company experiencing severe financial difficulties due to a lack of work and its forced closure. *Lion* was therefore dismantled at AEI's Attercliffe site, the engine being returned to Vickers at Barrow-in-Furness, where it had been built. AEI recovered its components and the bodyshell was scrapped by T. W. Ward.

A January 1964 report gave an overall satisfactory rating. Only one complete failure had occurred, while there had been two instances of severe delay, one due to train-heating boiler problems and the other to engine sump leakage. The bogies had given a hard ride, which may have caused cracking. While the electrical machines had not given trouble (except as noted), long-term experience with BR's Class 25, which had the same traction motors, found that these components were not entirely satisfactory through being highly rated — in the *Lion* application they were being asked to handle 50% more power and it seems highly likely that these components would have given trouble in squadron service. Of course, the Sulzer 12LDA28C engine suffered crankcase failures when installed in the BR/Brush Type 4 D1500s, resulting in a derating to 2,580bhp, so if *Lion* had been replicated, the same difficulty would have arisen. No D0260 ran 80,000 miles and this led some to re-christen it 'White Elephant' instead of 'White Lion'.

D0260 *Lion*	
Length	63ft 6in
Width	8ft 10in
Height	12ft 9¾in
Weight	114 tons
Wheel diameter	3ft 9in
Engine	Sulzer 12LDA28C
Engine output	2,750bhp at 800rpm
Maximum speed	100mph
Tractive effort, maximum	55,000lb
continuous	30,000lb at 25.5mph
Gear ratio	70:17
Fuel tank capacity	850 gallons
Minimum curve radius	4 chains
Works Number DEL260	

7 HS4000 Kestrel

The single-engined 2,700bhp diesel-electric locomotives of the early 1960s pushed the DC main generator to its limit of commutation, beyond which these electrical machines became prone to flashover. Improvements in technology, however, came along at just the right time to meet BR's aspirations for higher-powered locomotives. Chapter 2 dealt with the pioneering work that Brush was carrying out on the use of both electronics and AC power generation, and this helped

in the development of a single-engined traction unit of much higher power than hitherto. Studies had shown that this arrangement was more economical in terms of initial capital cost, maintenance and fuel consumption than either a multi-engined locomotive (such as *Deltic*) or a master-and-slave combination of locomotives. A further factor in the equation was that Sulzer had developed an uprated version of its LVA24 diesel. In 16-cylinder form, this passed the UIC

The great bulk of the Sulzer 16LVA24 engine and Brush traction alternator being lowered into the HS4000 bodyshell. *Brush*

After a handing-over ceremony at Marylebone on 30 January 1968, No HS4000 *Kestrel* made a demonstration run to Princes Risborough, where it is seen on arrival. *Ian Allan Library*

rating test at 4,000 metric horsepower (3,946bhp), operating at 1,100rpm.

Until the contents of archived files were recently made public, the *Kestrel* project had been assumed as a Hawker Siddeley/Sulzer speculative joint venture. The former, of course, owned Brush, and would have been the ultimate arbiter in allocating capital for the venture. While this was clearly the case, it is now also evident that the BRB played a major part in the design. By 1965 J. F. Harrison (by then effectively the BR CME), who has featured in other decisions concerning locomotive developments in this book, appreciated that there would come a time when a 4,000bhp traction unit would be required. The ER was also interested in exploring the possibility of a 'Super Deltic' of more than 4,000bhp to enable speed to be raised above 100mph.

The *Kestrel* project — the name being that given to the locomotive on completion — was under way by 1965 as Brush Contract No 04/20700. No manufacturer would produce a prototype that BR would not allow to operate on its metals, so some collaboration with the railway was essential. Both Brush and

Sulzer would also be keen to gain export business, so the final product would need to offer wide appeal. Taking account of BR's planned future requirements would help ensure that the design was as forward-looking as possible. Set against this background, it is unsurprising that BR had an input into the design process.

Construction of the locomotive was undertaken at Falcon Works, with the Sulzer diesel built in France, rather than Vickers, which had supplied the 12LDA28C units for the BR/Brush Type 4. A Brush BL120-50 AC traction generator was used, rated at 2,520kW at 1,100rpm. Brush fitted a BL63-38 combined auxiliary and train supply generator, which operated through a step-up gearbox at 2.5 times engine speed and had a maximum output of 530kVa at 1,100rpm engine speed. It incorporated an AC exciter to avoid the need for slip rings and brushes. After being rectified from AC to DC, power from the traction alternator was supplied to six Brush TM73-68 Mark 4 traction motors, which were a development of those first used in BR Classes 31 and 46. These motors had two stages of field weakening, were

connected in all-parallel, and were rated at 830A, 522V, 531hp at 681rpm, using a gear ratio of 60:19.

Brush opted for a Co-Co wheel arrangement on bogies of the Commonwealth pattern, which the company had used previously in its Type 2 and 4 designs. The traction motors were axle-hung, one per axle. The calculated performance characteristic offered full power between around 18mph and 100mph, and a continuous top speed of 110mph, though the maximum service speed was 125mph and the design top speed was 130mph. Maximum tractive effort was 70,000lb, and the continuous tractive effort was 41,200lb at 27.5mph. Clearly HS4000, the locomotive's BR running number, was designed for mixed traffic duties because the continuous top speed was, perhaps, a little low, while the continuous rating speed of 27.5mph was high for heavy freight deployment. Sanding gear was fitted, an interesting shift back to 1950s practice after abandonment of the facility with the large Type 4s.

Just as English Electric used DP2 as a test bed for a full electronic control system, Brush did likewise with No HS4000. This facilitated a wheelslip detection and correction system that offered a rapid response, as well as a driver's vigilance device in preference to the traditional 'deadman's pedal'. Dynamic braking was included. Interestingly, Brush chose an air management system that employed inertial filters, which followed prevailing USA practice in being of the roof-mounted, pendant type.

For the bodyshell Brush followed the same stressed-skin pattern as had been used on its Type 4s. The overall length, at 66ft 6in, was only 3 feet longer than the previous design. The cab front was semi-streamlined and incorporated a wrap-around Triplex windscreen — this was proposed by English Electric for the Class 50 design, but rejected by BR, so anyone wishing to visualise how that class might have looked should reflect on the pictures here of No HS4000! A two-tone exterior livery of yellow (upper) and chocolate brown (lower) was chosen, with silver-grey for the roof.

Care was taken with the locomotive's internal layout to reduce maintenance

After the initial formalities were over, the locomotive commenced a series of trials. On 8 May 1968 it passes Wigan North Western en route from Crewe to Carlisle.
David Wharton

times. Components were designed to require minimal maintenance or were positioned for maximum access, and it was estimated that this would save a third of the maintenance time needed for one of the Brush Type 4s. The cab environment was considered to be good: instrumentation and the layout of the driver's controls were well planned, while the inertial filter pressurising fan brought the added benefit of a slightly pressurised cab atmosphere that reduced draughts.

The design weight was for a 21-ton axle load, 126 tons in total. However, when No HS4000 made its first main-line run to Derby for weighing on 20 January 1968, the actual weight turned out to be 133 tons. A ceremony was conducted at Marylebone nine days later, with the Hawker Siddeley, Brush and BR chairmen in attendance. This was followed by a demonstration run to Princes Risborough and back, 36 miles each way, with six coaches.

A couple of months prior to these events, Hawker Siddeley's Chairman wrote to his opposite number at BR. This was not only both a 'thankyou' letter for help provided by BR's technical staff during the design work, but also a request for assistance with publicity and trial running. While he was naturally hoping for some commitment from BR that it would be interested in buying a production version of *Kestrel*, the latter's Chairman felt unable to oblige. He was willing to assist with publicity to win export orders, but emphasised that the Board was re-evaluating its future traction needs. As history shows, this quickly brought a shift away from large mixed-traffic locomotives to specialised motive power, such as the power cars for the High Speed Train.

Internal politics within BR arose as to where *Kestrel* should be handed over. No HS4000 was to be trialled on the ER, and its General Manager wanted the hand-over ceremony to be at King's Cross. A demonstration run thereafter would be able to operate at high speed and there would be minimal inconvenience in providing footplate crews compared with a launch at Marylebone. Further, a high-speed demonstration run from the latter station was not practical. In the event, Brush requested Marylebone because it felt there would be a better turnout from BR Board members.

After the hand-over and demonstration run, *Kestrel* returned to Falcon Works to await the start of its trials. After evaluating the overweight situation, made worse by uneven loading on the axles, the ER Civil Engineer pronounced his unwillingness to sanction a maximum speed above 75mph, whereas 90 had previously been envisaged.

Test running took place during the spring of 1968. While hauling a 650-ton train between Crewe and Carlisle, Shap summit was topped at 46mph, the speed that a 2,700bhp Type 4 would have achieved, but with a 200-ton lighter trailing load. When running with No 1 end leading, the engine room became excessively hot, while exhaust gases were drawn inside the locomotive; fitting baffles inside the engine room resolved the problem. No other major problems were reported, so the trials appear to have been successful.

Meanwhile the BR Chief Civil Engineer had been carrying out research into the effect on the track of stresses caused by the arrangement of mounting traction motors on bogie axles. As a result, for 100mph running a maximum axle load of 20 tons was laid down, and No HS4000 exceeded this by a considerable margin, which thwarted the ambitions for deployment on high-speed passenger duties. BR was allegedly rather embarrassed by the way the situation with this prototype had turned out. The Board had been a key player in the project and Brush was keen to get as much publicity from No HS4000's activities as possible, if not for a domestic order, then possibly overseas. At that time it was the most powerful single-engined locomotive in the world.

BR relented to Brush pressure and agreed to accept what was rapidly turning into a financial white elephant for freight duties, which would have to be confined to rosters that could be performed by a single running depot in order to minimise train crew familiarisation. Although nominally allocated to Tinsley from 14 May 1968, No HS4000 was outbased at Shirebrook, where it was assigned a Brush Class 47 diagram, commencing on the 15th. This comprised two return trips each weekday between Mansfield and Whitemoor Yard, hauling coal trains with a gross weight of between 1,450 and 1,600 tons. Heavier loads were impractical due to the limits imposed by loops and sidings, whilst the wagons had a maximum permitted speed of 35mph. All in all, therefore, this operating regime was not taxing for so powerful a machine. During one measured daily cycle, 19 hours were spent in operation but a mere 6 minutes on full power.

More testing was conducted during August 1968. On the 11th runs were made between Derby, Crewe and Nuneaton at speeds of up to 102mph. AC electric No E3122 was used to add to the overall train weight by use of its dynamic brake. The electric locomotive was also used to tow the train, with No HS4000 at the rear, to test the latter's dynamic brake. A tractive effort of 85,900lb was recorded at 10.3mph, which, while considerably above the predicted maximum of 66,000lb, only represented 2,360 rhp, a disappointingly low figure. Taken together with other runs, it seems that the traction alternator was delivering 3,340hp, or 83% of the rated engine output, whereas the Brush Class 47 achieved an 89% efficiency figure. The latter then lost only 10% of the generator output in the traction motors, a typical figure for a diesel-electric. If this percentage is applied to No HS4000's generator output of 3,340hp, then one would have expected around 3,000rhp. With six traction motors, each rated continuously at 515hp, 3,090hp in total, this performance should have been attained, yet nothing has come to light to suggest that the locomotive managed it.

Later that month a demonstration heavy-haul trial took place between

No HS4000 *Kestrel* first saw service use on coal trains between North Nottinghamshire collieries and Whitemoor Yard, and it is pictured here on a typical coal duty during 1968. *Brush*

Mansfield and Lincoln, the 2,028-ton trailing load just exceeding the previous heaviest, which had been handled by a Great Western Railway 2-8-0 steam locomotive more than half a century previously. Restarting the train on a 1 in 150 incline, where the rails were wet, three-quarter setting of the power controller caused some wheelslip, but allowed an acceleration to 15mph in 7 minutes. A minor spin-off for Brush from the success of No HS4000's system was the ordering of 100 electronic control systems for Class 47.

After attention at Falcon Works, the prototype was back at work on Shirebrook coal turns from 22 November, and this pattern continued until 2 April 1969. By the end of 1968, 26,000 miles had been run, 22,000 in revenue service.

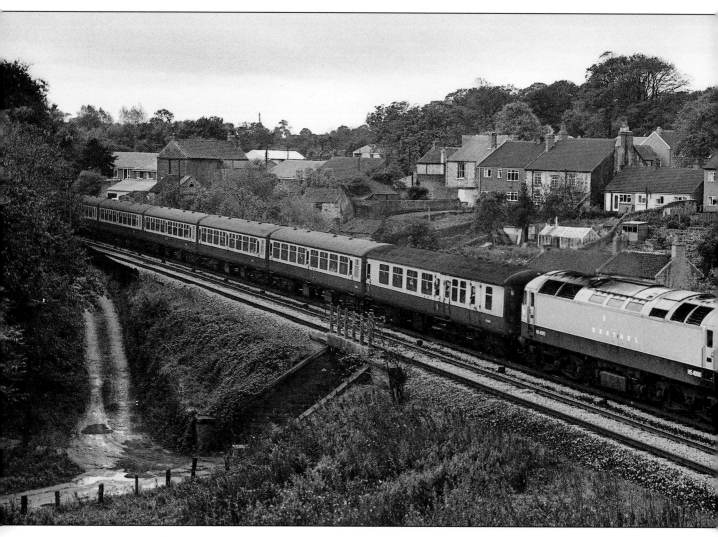

Enthusiasts lean out of the leading carriage windows to savour No HS4000's sound to full effect as it heads the 08.00 King's Cross to Newcastle service past Aycliffe, County Durham, on 25 October 1969. *John M. Boyes*

With a view to reducing weight from an unacceptable 23 tons to 20 tons per axle, No HS4000 returned to Brush for a set of Class 47 bogies to be fitted, which then permitted 100mph passenger duties to be assigned.

Returning to the main line by mid-June 1969, this time based at King's Cross, a 'Deltic' diagram was assigned after crew training had been completed by October. Typically, No HS4000 went down to Newcastle on the 07.55, a fast but lightly loaded train that was booked for only eight coaches. The return leg was on the 16.45 to London. A sighting was reported in April 1970 on a King's Cross to Hull freightliner. A published log on the down service saw the 232¼ miles to Darlington run in 191min 12sec, 2½ minutes late on schedule, although the net running time

(after deducting signal and track slowings) was only 173½ minutes. Attempting to recover lost time, the driver took liberties with the upper speed limit: north of York, between Tollerton and Danby Wiske, 24 miles were reeled off at an average of 102.3mph, top speed being 107. Assessing the power output during the journey is difficult because of the short duration when full power was used. Estimates in three locations suggest around 2,750rhp, a figure barely above a standard 'Deltic' level and well below the theoretical figure for *Kestrel*. These estimates reinforce the low output recorded during the initial tests already referred to. Was the locomotive derated? We shall probably never know.

No HS4000 then spent some time at Vickers, Barrow, for an engine

and was used (no doubt among other work) on international passenger services to Bucharest, capital of Romania.

From the standpoint of its tractive power, No HS4000 was about 15 years ahead of its time, because Foster Yeoman demonstrated with its Class 59s that heavy payloads of more than 4,600 tons could be hauled with a single traction unit. Of course, one should not forget that the Sulzer LVA24 diesel did not prove to be a conspicuous success in the five examples of the Brush Type 4 (Class 48) in which it was installed in 12-cylinder form. Curiously, English Electric acquired a licence to manufacture the LVA24, possibly as an alternative to its own RK range, but no commercial application emerged from the arrangement. Brush demonstrated the capability of its first main-line AC power generation system and this, no doubt, helped it win the order for the equipment used in Class 56. No HS4000's bogies did not give a good ride and lessons were learned that were later applied in Class 56. Perhaps if a four-axle bogie had been used, the axle load would have been within the prescribed 20-ton limit for 100mph passenger work. No DP2 and *Falcon* certainly enjoyed a much more diverse and strenuous operating regime than No HS4000 during its days on the East Coast route.

examination. The prototype emerged on 2 September and returned to Shirebrook. However, with no prospect of an order for a fleet based on the design, Brush sold No HS4000 to the Soviet Union, although Germany also expressed an interest in it. *Kestrel* was taken out of traffic in either February or March 1971 for modification at Crewe Works, including alterations for the broader Soviet rail gauge. With the work completed, on 5 June it was seen on Crewe depot in readiness for movement to Cardiff and shipment to Russia. This took place on 8 July through Cardiff Docks, movement to the port being on Class 47 bogies. It was originally thought that *Kestrel* was dismantled for technological appraisal, but more recently *Modern Railways* carried a report about its fate: it survived, in fact, until 1989,

No HS4000 *Kestrel*	
Length	66ft 6in
Width	8ft 9¾in
Height	13ft 0½in
Weight	133 tons
Wheel diameter	3ft 7in
Engine	Sulzer 16LVA24
Engine output	4,000bhp
Maximum speed	125mph
Tractive effort, maximum	70,000lb
Gear ratio, original	60:19
revised	53:18
Fuel tank capacity	1,000 gallons
Minimum curve radius	4 chains

Works Number 711 of 1967

8

The Type 5 Prototype

As the so-called Oil Crisis of 1973 brought a need for greater reliance on coal for electricity generation, so also arose a pressing need for suitable traction for handling the railborne transit of this fuel. Of course No HS4000 *Kestrel* had only just been sold to the USSR, while BR's fleet lacked the capacity to fulfil the anticipated extra demand. BR therefore drew up an outline specification for a freight locomotive, with a top speed of 80mph but capable of handling heavy trains without exceeding its continuous

rating, as had happened when Class 47 was put initially on enhanced MGR workings. Horsepower in the 3,000-3,500 range was envisaged. The eventual order to Brush specified the use of, basically, a Class 47-style locomotive, but using a new power train, control and auxiliaries. The changes featured AC power generation and control as demonstrated in No HS4000, while a 16CSVT engine from GEC (into which EE had merged) would provide the power.

A Mark 3 version of the 16CSVT unit

Photos of No D47601 are rare. On 28 February 1977 it is a little smoky as it gets under way from Treeton Junction, near Sheffield. Note that it still looks reasonably 'ex-works'. *G. W. Morrison*

fitted in Class 50 had been produced while that class was still under construction. The resultant diesel benefited from, among other improvements, oil-cooled pistons and a gear drive (in place of chain) for the camshafts. The rating for what GEC termed the 16RK3CT was now 3,520bhp at 900rpm, but BR opted for a setting of 3,250bhp at 900rpm. (In fact, this was really not the correct nomenclature for this engine, because the 'V' range was a development of the 'RK' range. During the various amalgamations of the 1960s that involved EE, Harry Watson, a non-EE man, had become head of diesel interests and had merged the two ranges into one under the 'RK' heading. In strict EE parlance, the new diesel should have been the 16CSVT Mark 3.)

BR wished to try out the main components of the power train in advance of the production locomotives being built, and selected a Class 47 to serve as a test bed. Space precludes a detailed description as to why No 47046 was selected, together with the extent of the modifications made, but within it was installed a 16RK3CT engine, serial number IH 8116 (GEC Diesels Contract No 734/40382), coupled to a Brush BA1101A traction alternator. Accommodating the new power train and associated auxiliary control equipment posed quite a design headache and helped slow down the project. To distinguish the changeling, in December 1975 it was renumbered to 47601 and was allocated to Tinsley, where the first of the new freight design, Class 56, was to be based.

Regrettably, the return-to-traffic date has proved elusive, but it was demonstrated at Tinsley in the company of No 56001 on 9 November 1976. This meant that the plan to trial the new equipment had been lost. ER management seems not to have been keen on the prototype because of the limited operational flexibility caused by its non-standard features, and the need for training footplate and depot staff. Photographic evidence shows deployment on MGR coal traffic around South Yorkshire, and when the time came for it to be fitted with a new GEC diesel, the ER declined to accept it back.

This view finds No D47601 at Treeton South Sidings on the same day. *L. A. Nixon*

BR was planning a new freight Type 5 design, Class 58, and wished to try the GEC Diesels 12RK3ACT unit, rated at 3,300bhp at 1,000rpm. In September 1978 No 47601 went back to Crewe Works for a second conversion, just about two years after the first. A further renumbering took place in November 1979, this time to No 47901, which was a prelude to release from Crewe the following month. Engine IH 8116 was replaced by prototype 12RK3ACT No IH 8624 under GEC Diesels Contract No 634/80564. During trials under the auspices of the Railway Technical Centre at Derby, a camshaft cover failed during January 1980 and caused a return to Crewe for repair. Out-shopped on 30 May,

Right: Still in Rail Blue, but converted to a Class 47/9, No 47901 thrashes up Upton Scudamore bank near Warminster on 26 July 1988 with the 12.09 Whatley-Fareham ARC train. No 37227 gives banking assistance. *John Chalcraft*

Below: No D47901 made hardly any appearances on passenger trains. On 1 July 1984 it was requested by F & W Railtours for its 'Skeggy Bucketeer' rail tour, seen here storming out of Bristol at Dr Days Bridge Junction. *Chris Holland*

it was returned to traffic on 13 June. Despite crews not being trained on the machine, the LMR made use of it for a time because it was noted at Birkenhead Mollington Street depot on the 19th.

The WR agreed to accept No 47901 and it was allocated initially to Cardiff Canton. At first it was put to use on steel traffic, but changing patterns quickly saw a forced redeployment on coal imported through Cardiff, operated by an Ebbw Junction locomotive. This again proved short-lived, but when the importation ceased No 47901 remained at Ebbw Junction for steel traffic. After a period hauling stone from Tytherington Quarry to Wolverton, the locomotive moved to Bristol Bath Road on 3 October 1982, where it was out-based at Westbury for the Mendip quarry stone movements.

When the Railfreight Sector pulled out of Bath Road, No 47901 was transferred to Canton from November 1987, where it remained until withdrawal on 23 March 1990 — arrival of Class 59, first used by Foster Yeoman and later by ARC, made the prototype redundant. It had been nominally 'written off' as a developmental machine several times during the previous decade, but GEC kept coming back to it as different engine problems beset Class 58, which were not

manifested in No 47901. In fact, it had been uprated to 3,500bhp not long after arrival at Ebbw Junction, but this was kept quiet to avoid any demands from the drivers' union for higher pay.

The engine itself gave no trouble, though associated pipework was a source of problems. Being non-standard, this meant long periods dumped at Bath Road awaiting replacement parts. Surprisingly, the standard Class 47 traction motors gave no trouble, despite the substantial extra current being supplied to them. It was a remarkable performer among the prototypes.

Above: On 16 April 1988 No 47901 coasts past Newbury Racecourse with the 10.45 SO Thorney Mill-Merehead train, a typical Westbury Class 56 diagram on which the Class 47/9 was deployed. *Mark Few*

Left: Bursting out of Fisherton Tunnel east of Salisbury, No 47901 takes the junction road with the 12.03 Westbury to Fareham train on 20 July 1989. *Chris Holland*

9

Locomotives Used as Engine Test Beds

No D830 *Majestic*

During construction of the production series of Swindon Class 42 diesel-hydraulics, a decision was taken to install an engine of a new design from the Paxman stable. That company had announced the new design in January 1959, which was aimed at rivalling those products available on the Continent. Known as the 'YJ' or 'Ventura', it was designed to deliver up to 1,500bhp in 12-cylinder form at 1,500rpm. BR was content for testing to proceed and it was arranged that one of the production Class 42s under construction at Swindon would have two 12YJXL units fitted in place of the two Maybach diesels. For BR service a rating of 1,135bhp at 1,530rpm was adopted, identical to the other Class 42s. The resulting locomotive, No D830, weighed 77 tons 6cwt, more than a ton less than its classmates, but otherwise it was the same.

No D830 entered traffic on 19 January 1961 and was based initially at Plymouth Laira before moving to Newton Abbot.

In what the photographer describes as non-standard blue livery, No D830 *Majestic* has been on an inter-regional working, judging by the headcode, on 15 May 1967.
C. H. S. Owen

The engines performed very well, no doubt helped by the presence of a Paxman riding technician, but also because there were no major design flaws. An operating sphere was arranged that ensured out-and-back diagrams off Newton Abbot, with the Kingswear to Paddington 'Torbay Express' being a regular duty.

The crankshafts fitted gave some trouble, causing engine failure, and were replaced by an enhanced design. A failure of this component first occurred during February 1964, but when the replacement item also failed during October 1968, No D830 was stored until it was withdrawn on 26 March 1969, an inevitable move because all the Class 42 and 43 fleet were entering their run-down phase. In 7 years 9 months of service, the locomotive ran roughly 447,000 miles, a low annual average caused by time out of traffic awaiting repair, the curse of all prototypes.

The venture had some commercial spin-offs for Paxman. As noted in Chapter 5, 20 NBL Class 21s received the same engine in place of their MAN units, with a rating in this application of 1,350bhp at 1,500rpm. In six-cylinder form, the 'Ventura' was installed in the BR Swindon Class 14 and Class 74 electro-diesels.

Class 48

Sulzer recognised that its 12LDA28C represented the practical limit for development of the twin-bank type of medium-speed engine, due to constraints on engine room space and axle loading. Nevertheless, the demand from railway operators for more power continued and in 1958 French National Railways prompted Sulzer to develop a new range of high-performance diesels. Advances in bearing technology made the company less cautious about using a 'V' form of cylinder arrangement, so the LVA24 range was conceived, with a 24cm cylinder bore, rather than 28cm, and running at a maximum of 1,050rpm. French National Railways ordered a series of locomotives with 12LVA24 engines, nominally rated at 2,650bhp at 1,050rpm, and these first appeared in May 1963.

By then J. F. Harrison, a Sulzer devotee, had become Chief Engineer, Traction & Rolling Stock, on BR, and he was interested to evaluate the new power unit. Brush was building 25 Class 47s under a contract awarded in September 1962, and it was agreed that the last five of these would receive 12LVA24 units in place of the standard 12LDA28C. The new engine weighed 15.2 tons, a saving of 6.5 tons. A Mark 5 version of the Brush

By September 1967 No D830 had been repainted with full yellow ends, and is seen here at Dawlish Warren on an Exeter St Davids to Paignton local. *N. E. Preedy*

TG160-60 main generator, fitted in Mark 4 form in Class 47, was used, continuously rated at 1,742kW, 818V, 2,130A. The traction motors were the same as Class 47 but with a 14hp lower continuous rating at 354hp, while road performance was, theoretically, almost identical.

As is inevitably the case with new designs, extra time was needed to make the necessary arrangements, so the first Class 48 did not enter traffic until 17 September 1965, some 20 months after the last conventional Class 47 from the same order. Numbered D1702-6, initial allocation was to Tinsley depot, Sheffield, from where their principal deployment was on coal traffic, working off Shirebrook depot. Rather than train all footplate crews, diagramming was on an out-and-back basis, which explains appearances on the 'Sheffield Pullman' and 'Master Cutler' turn, with two return trips to King's Cross.

With a view to greater passenger work being assigned, a migration to the Great Eastern Section commenced in December 1968, where No D1705 appeared on the 21st. Re-allocation to Norwich Thorpe

Above left: **While based at Tinsley, Class 48 had a regular passenger diagram that involved two return trips between Sheffield Midland and King's Cross. No D1704 makes a fine sight passing Knebworth with the seven-coach 19.20 down 'Master Cutler' on 29 May 1968.** *David Percival*

Left: **When based in East Anglia, Class 48's stamping ground was on Liverpool Street to Norwich duties. On 30 June 1969 No D1703 crosses a DMU at Ardleigh in charge of the 17.40 up service.** *G. R. Mortimer*

Above: **In July 1969 No D1704 awaits its next turn of duty at Norwich depot.** *N. E. Preedy*

Class 37/9s made regular appearances on the North & West route as part of their Metals Sector duties. No D37901 *Mirrlees Pioneer* approaches Shrewsbury with the 11.25 Dee Marsh Junction to Margam train. *David N. Clough*

depot did not come until June 1969, followed in October by a move to Stratford, then back to Tinsley in February 1970.

From new, Sulzer deployed technicians at both Tinsley and Shirebrook to assist with the care of the diesels. These personnel no doubt helped deal with initial issues and kept locomotives operational that might otherwise have been failures. Nevertheless, even they could not address a fundamental weakness that caused crankshaft failures

on four of the five engines due to bearing problems. No D1702 was laid up from September 1968, when it was noted in Crewe Works' arrival sidings on the 29th; it languished in Crewe until completion of work to convert it to a standard Class 47 in February 1970. The remainder were then taken out of service and dealt with in similar fashion. The redundant engines from Class 48 were sold back to their French builder and, after refurbishment, these were sold on for use in locomotives in France.

National Railways had experienced the same difficulty and resolved it, but failed to pass on the information. Had it done so, the Class 48s might have enjoyed a much longer and more successful career, with the LVA24 engine proving to be a serious competitor to GEC Diesel's Mark 3 CSVT range.

This is, of course, speculation, and one needs to remember that EE had acquired manufacturing rights for the LVA24. Whether this was to gain access to the associated engineering technology to help improve its CSVT range, or whether EE actually did intend to produce Sulzer diesels under licence, will probably never be known. Some have said that the 12LVA24s could have been the preferred power unit for what became Class 50. As its troubles had not emerged by the time EE was well down the road of producing the Class 50 design, this option seems unlikely, though it is an interesting thought. If EE had abandoned its CSVT range in favour of the LVA24, then what is about to be described in the next section would have been completely different!

Class 37/9

In February 1985 GEC Diesels asked BR for facilities to try its new Ruston RK270T diesel. No doubt tipped off about this, a few months later the Hawker Siddeley Group (of which Brush and Mirrlees were subsidiaries) made a similar approach for its Mirrlees Blackstone MB275T unit. Undoubtedly both manufacturers had in mind BR's plans for a new freight design of between 1,800 and 2,100bhp, coded Class 38, and the Class 37 Life Extension Programme, which was in full swing at Crewe Works at the time. This offered an ideal opportunity for test-bed locomotive conversions.

This is not the place to describe the work being carried out on the Class 37s undergoing life extension, but both GEC and Brush were supplying traction alternators and associated equipment as part of the scheme. Under the programme several subclasses were being created, one of which was a 'heavyweight' freight type in which ballast was added to give a total

There is a sad end to this story. At the time of the bearing failures, both BR and Sulzer blamed each other. When No HS4000's engine, a 16-cylinder version of the LVA24, also failed for the same reason, Sulzer carried out a more thorough investigation, and found that a tool used to fit the bearing shells had a locating pin that was slightly out of position. This meant that the shells were incorrectly fitted and high spots occurred that, by a chain of events, caused crankshaft failure. Ironically, French

Above: The class also usually covered the steel coil services between Crewe Gresty Lane and Cardiff Tidal Sidings, which started from Mossend New Yard. On 3 May 1989 No D37905 *Vulcan Enterprise* slogs upgrade through Church Stretton with the 06.35 train from Mossend. *David N. Clough*

Right: Showing off its Railfreight Metals Sector livery, No D37902 *British Steel Llanwern* poses for the camera at Gloucester on 4 August 1991. *N. E. Preedy*

No D37906 approaches Gloucester on 5 July 1993 powering the Scunthorpe to Cardiff Tidal Sidings train. *N. E. Preedy*

locomotive weight of 120 tons to increase adhesion. It was this heavyweight variant that was selected as the type into which the new engines should be put.

Substituting one of the replacement power units for the standard 12CSVT should, therefore, have presented less of a challenge. As with No 47601, however, the design work did prove difficult, primarily in order to accommodate an engine silencer of sufficient size to reduce external noise levels to the relevant UIC standards. Originally the conversions were proposed to be carried out at Falcon and Vulcan Works respectively, but, as neither was rail-connected, Crewe did the job instead.

GEC's 6RK270T was rated at up to 2,400bhp, but was set to deliver 1,800bhp at 900rpm for consistency with other class members, and the two conversions made use of GEC alternators. No 37905 was fitted with engine No IH 9711 and No 37906 with IH 9710. Mirrlees offered four 6MB275T engines for evaluation, these being set at 1,800bhp at 1,000rpm. Brush traction alternators and associated equipment were matched to these prime movers. The Railfreight Sector had agreed to accept the locomotives as part of its allocation and decided to base the sextet at Canton, where they could be deployed with minimum driver training.

Running numbers 37901-4 were used for the Mirrlees-fitted examples, and Nos 37905-6 for the GEC ones.

Deliveries took place between October 1986 and April 1987, during which period several trial runs had been staged over the North & West route to Dee Marsh and between Port Talbot and Llanwern. The latter saw two Class 37/9s handle a standard 3,060-tonne load of iron ore that would be diagrammed for two Class 56s in multiple. Intensive diagramming was envisaged and figures for 1988 saw an average of 2,100 TOPS hours per locomotive, whereas a WR Class 56 averaged only 1,700. After some slight problems with the alternators and control equipment associated with the Mirrlees engines, both types settled down to give very satisfactory performance.

While the Class 38 project proved stillborn, the Mirrlees engine in eight-cylinder form was selected for use in Class 60. No 37901 was named *Mirrlees Pioneer*, No 37902 *British Steel Llanwern* and No 37905 *Vulcan Enterprise* — so, 25 years after DP2, Vulcan got to call a locomotive *Enterprise*! The operating regime remained largely unaltered, being generally Railfreight Metals duties until the latter days of service use. No 37901 never ran again after catching fire on 7 February 1995, while No 37902 was stored on 24 December 1998, eight days after No 37903. No 37904 appears to have been out of traffic since February 1995, but was purchased for preservation in September 2001. No 37905 was stored unserviceable on 7 January 1997, with No 37906 suffering a similar fate on 18 December 1996. Both are part of the EWS Heritage Fleet and the latter has been used at several diesel galas on preserved railways.

About 18 months before its main-line service ended, on 29 May 1997, No 37903, eases through Newport with the 10.10 Margam to Llanwern train. *N. E. Preedy*